THE MEAT MACHINE

JAN WALSH

THE
MEAT MACHINE

*The inside story of the
meat business*

COLUMBUS BOOKS
LONDON

First published in Great Britain in 1986 by
Columbus Books Limited
19-23 Ludgate Hill, London EC4M 7PD

Designed by Fred Price
Illustrations by Val Hill

British Library Cataloguing in Publication Data
Walsh, Jan
The meat machine.
1. Meat——Quality   2. Meat industry and trade——Great
Britain
——Quality control
I. Title
664'.907   TS1975

ISBN 0-86287-294-4

Phototypeset by Falcon Graphic Art Ltd
Wallington, Surrey
Printed and bound by
Mackays of Chatham Ltd, Kent

FOR MY TASTERS . . .
MIKE, MICHELLE AND BAILEY

Contents

Introduction

'Meat's got the lot!' That advertising slogan of the mid-'eighties now has a sinister ring for many of us. The hormones scare, concern over additives and, more lately, worries about the antibiotics being pumped into livestock, have given the meat industry's much-used phrase an unfortunate double meaning.

But meat includes far more 'ingredients' than we would ever imagine. What we think of as meat and what the industry *calls* meat are two very different things. From the birth of a calf to the selling of a steak pie, right down the line, the meat machine is at work to maximize profits by converting every possible part of the carcass into something edible. Along the way the meat may be given doses not only of hormones and antibiotics, but tranquillizers and tenderizers, too.

Most of us have no idea what happens on the farm, where the meat machine gets its raw materials. We may fondly imagine our food animals roaming free, fattening themselves on rolling green pastureland. But the best pasture is reserved for dairy cattle nowadays. Almost all pigs and chickens, and some cattle, are raised intensively, in indoor units. Even lambs are reared by factory-farm methods. The farmer's greatest concern is to get a quick return on his capital. In days gone by he might have waited three years before sending his cattle to market. Now he needs to send them at two years or under to make the biggest profits. Hormonal growth-promoters have given him the ability to speed up nature, but they have also caused the greatest outcry from consumers. It is a fascinating argument. On the farmers' side, scientists insist that any hormone residues in meat cannot possibly do

9

us any harm. But most consumers prefer to follow their instincts and avoid eating hormones. Whom does the government support? It backs the farmers, though it has been forced to follow an EEC call for a ban on hormones.

While everyone has been getting very heated over hormones, another factory-farming method, which could have far more dangerous repercussions, has gone virtually unnoticed until now. Farmers have taken to dosing their animals with drugs – often the same drugs that are used in human medicine. Because the unnatural conditions of intensive rearing units spread disease like wildfire, farmers have been forced to give their livestock antibiotics to keep them healthy. Some animals develop aggressive behaviour in their overcrowded conditions and have to be tranquillized to ensure they continue to put on weight. The more nature is abused, the more she will strike back.

The well-oiled cogs of the meat machine have been turning in our slaughterhouses, too, but this time in virtual silence. In the pursuit of extra-tender meat, some cattle have to suffer the distress of being boxed up, having their heads pulled high, and enduring a long injection of a tenderizing enzyme. This treatment has nothing to do with the animals' health, but a lot to do with the health of the industry's profits. Despite an official report which condemned the treatment, the company concerned has managed to carry on without attracting any public outcry. And although there is no excuse for this objectionable practice, the government has so far refused to take action.

Other problems in slaughterhouses have been virtually ignored as well, and we are to blame. Until now most of us have preferred not to think too deeply about how our food animals are killed. We skirt round the issue in our minds, hoping that the official watchdogs will see that the process is humane, preferring not to know if it is not. The fact is that if we accept that it is justifiable to kill animals for food – and since there are less than a million true vegetarians in Britain, most of us must – then we have a duty to take an interest in how it is done. The minders of the meat machine would prefer us to stay in blissful ignorance because there is much to hide. It *is* however possible, and easy, to slaughter animals humanely, but only concern and pressure from a great many people will ensure that methods are used which do not inflict needless distress.

In the factory the meat machine gets into top gear. Here the recipes are all-important. A minute change in the amount of lean meat used can mean the difference between profit and loss. Processed meat may be mixed with fat, rind, gristle and sinew, and the whole unhealthy mixture may be passed off quite legally as meat. Discarded bones are often pounded for every ounce of flesh, or more likely sinew, which clings to them. Blood and bones are added on occasion to bulk out the meat, it is believed. Time and again science has come up with new ways to make that very precious commodity stretch further. But of all the tricks commonly employed, pumping meat until it is full of water must be the worst.

Conmen may daydream about selling nothing for something . . . but some meat manufacturers do it every day. They put water in ham, bacon, cooked meats and raw roasting joints, and charge us for the privilege of buying it. They inject the meat through banks of pincushion-like needles until it can be seen to swell, then they tumble it in a giant machine until chemicals persuade the meat cells to hang on to all the extraneous water.

The recipes used by manufacturers would surprise most of us. An ordinary pork pie, for instance, will probably contain little more than 10 per cent recognizable pork flesh, and even that is likely to be head meat. The ingredients list gives no hint of this. The meat machine can cover its tracks when it needs to, and many less wholesome bits of the carcass may be disguised on the label by clever terminology.

The nuts and bolts of the whole contraption are colourings and flavourings. Without them, the machine would fall apart as the pasty, bland results of all the adulteration became obvious to the customer. Artificial colouring makes fatty sausages look meaty, and chemical flavouring gives watery ham a taste closer to that of the real thing.

Even when meat has reached the shops it is liable to tricks of the trade which have the effect of deceiving or misleading the customer. Cheap cuts may be passed off as more expensive pieces of meat. Padding and gas in the packaging can make the meat look more attractive. Even the display lighting may make the meat look fresher than it really is.

On the receiving end of all this adulteration and sharp practice are the 34 million people who eat meat – 98 per cent of the adult population. We enjoy meat and we recognize, as the advertising slogan quoted earlier intended to point out, that meat has got the lot in terms of first-class protein, carbohydrate, vitamins and minerals. Many of us feel deprived if we do not have a meat dish at least once a day, but at today's prices this is not always easy to afford. With well over half the household cooks out at work the trend is for convenient, low-cost meat products, particularly mid-week. For example, in 1984 we munched our way through 4,409 million sausages. That is 80 per person per year. Bacon and sausages are the two most popular meat dishes, bought every week by the vast majority of households. It is no coincidence that they are also the most adulterated products of all.

There is no end to the lengths some farmers, manufacturers and shops will go in their determination to capitalize on our desire to eat meat. But this book is not simply a guide to trickery. The decline of standards in processing our meat has far-reaching implications. What has happened is a steady adulteration of 'real meat'. But the process has been so slow and so subtle that at no point has anyone been able to call a halt. Only the government had that power, but in new regulations which came into force in July 1986, it has simply rubber-stamped all but the worst excesses.

As a result, we now have a number of meat products on the shop shelves which do not deserve their names. A slice of cured pork, for instance, may well have been made to soak up water like a sponge, may contain chemical polyphosphates, have been injected with flavour enhancer and packed with extra nitrites to make it look more pink. It is meant to be a delicious breakfast treat, but under the grill it spits and fizzles

12

as the water pours out, it oozes white gunge – caused by all the chemicals – and it ends up half its original size. The makers call it bacon . . . but it isn't.

Our grandmothers would not have touched such rubbish. They would have laughed till their sides split at the shrivelled offering in our frying-pans, and mocked us for our gullibility in buying it.

The government has now decided to give the makers of this watery imposter its official permission to continue calling it bacon . . . but that does not make it right. It has granted numerous similar practices its approval, with only one condition – the makers must own up to any extra ingredients on the pack. It is the equivalent of telling French wine producers that they may water down their Beaujolais as long as they label it 'with added water'.

What is worrying about the government's approach is that it shows a total disregard for the need to keep up the standards of our best-loved foods. If meat can be legally adulterated today, what will our butter, milk, fruit juice, scotch whisky, fish or cheese be like tomorrow? Already there are signs that standards are slipping in the production of some foods. If producers have taken note of what has happened in the meat industry they are unlikely to be deterred from using corner-cutting methods. Why should they . . . if one day the government will give them official approval?

But it is not all bad news. In one important area meat has had a raw deal. Think of diet, health and heart disease: most of us would immediately single out meat as arch enemy number one. But for all sorts of reasons meat has been unfairly subjected to criticism. It is not necessary to drop meat from your diet, or even to cut down on the number of meaty meals you serve, as long as the cuts are lean and trimmed of any hunks of obvious fat. There are even meats which are high in polyunsaturates. When have you ever heard that magic phrase 'high in polyunsaturates' used in reference to meat before?

This book is not intended to put anyone off eating meat,

though it may have that effect on a few. It is meant to make all of us realize how easily a good food can be devalued if its customers do not protest. The industry is bound to be rattled by what it will almost certainly view as yet another attack. But its more enlightened members may see that it can only be an encouraging sign for the British meat industry if its customers become more critical of unacceptable methods and poor quality. If the industry betrays our trust it may find, on the other hand, that the food that's got the lot will get the push.

1

The hidden additives

The countryside is no longer a place where nature reigns supreme. High technology has invaded the rolling pasturelands of Britain.

No more do our farm animals fatten themselves naturally on the grasses and grains they were designed to eat. Nowadays the farmer pumps them with drugs to make them plumper, healthier, and thus more profitable.

Beef cattle are given cocktails of hormones throughout their growing period, and sometimes up to the time of slaughter. Pigs, poultry, calves and dairy cows are dosed with antibiotics not only to keep disease at bay but also to promote maximum growth. During their overcrowded life, animals may be given shots of tranquillizer to keep them quiet. And as they near death they may be injected with an enzyme to make them tender.

Some of these drugs are a known danger to human health, yet they continue to be used for reasons of maximizing profit. Others have been given a clean bill of health by scientists who say we must trust their judgement.

Amazingly, no one is responsible for checking all the meat we eat to ensure it is uncontaminated by drugs. Animals cannot be tested on the farm because no method exists which can determine drug levels in the flesh while the animal is alive. In the slaughterhouse carcasses are checked by the local authority meat inspectors for disease, but their brief does not cover the residues of drugs. As a result a significant amount of 'drugged' meat may be reaching our dinner tables every day.

Ironically, the five hormones still in use for growth promotion have just passed a multi-million-pound research programme sponsored by the pharmaceuticals industry yet, in a rare victory for consumers, the EEC has banned them from use. The decision was due to take effect in the UK in 1989, but the government recently announced that it proposes to keep in step with its EEC partners and ban them from December 1986. They realise hormone-treated meat will soon be hard for our farmers to sell in Europe.

It is the instincts of consumers which have won the day. Although the farming industry is furious about the EEC's decision, the consumer attitude to hormone-treated meat is no more illogical than our attitude to horsemeat, or dogmeat. We do not *choose* to eat them and so there are laws which protect us from being served them unknowingly. The following explanation of the use of hormones will show that there are few grounds for real concern about them, but equally there is no justification at all for forcing consumers to accept them in the meat they buy.

Hormones are used to boost the animal's own growth secretions to make it put on weight faster, and in all the right places. They are almost always used on cattle, to beef up young steers and heifers, and to put some meat on the bones of worn-out dairy cows. Some sheep are also given hormones, especially lambs being grown on to a year old before slaughter. But it is not generally worth the farmer's while to inject other meat animals. Since the drugs take around three months to work and have set withdrawal times, pigs and poultry would go to market too young to gain any useful benefit.

Britain uses far more growth promoters than most other European countries. Only Belgium and Eire are likely to match our farmers' dependence on hormones to raise their cattle. It is not that our farmers are hooked on drugs. The reason is historical. In Britain we castrate our male cattle when they are only a few days old. The steers can then be safely grazed together in the fields until they are ready for slaughter at 15–18 months old.

On the continent, particularly in Denmark, Italy and West Germany, a group of young steers out at pasture is a rare sight. They keep their male calves 'entire' and as a result have

16

to raise them indoors in separate stalls to prevent fighting. The advantage of allowing bullocks to keep their vital parts is that they also keep their full quota of male hormones. A bullock will invariably be heavier at slaughter and provide more lean meat than a steer.

In Britain 'bull beef', as it is called, is only a small part of our production, although it is becoming more popular. The majority of our beef animals are steers and so to compete effectively with Europe our farmers feel they have to use hormones to put back what nature intended. That is why the EEC ban came as far more of a blow to British farmers than it did to the Continental countries.

According to Dr Alan Cooper of Seale-Hayne Agricultural College, 'With the reduced efficiencies of steers when compared to bulls, it is apparent that in the UK the potential for using growth-promoters, especially the subcutaneous implants, is probably greater than anywhere else in Europe.' Even bulls can benefit. According to Dr Cooper, when the synthetic female hormone Zeranol is used on bulls, 'it both retards sexual development and reduces sexual/aggressive behaviour, making implanted bulls much easier to manage'.

Of the five products on the market, three are known as 'natural' hormones and two are synthetic. But although the farming industry insists on using the word 'natural', it can be misleading. None of the hormones has been, as one might suppose, naturally extracted from any animal. One of the three, Compudose, is extracted from the soya bean without any further refinement, but the other two, Implixa and Synovex, are manufactured from chemicals. All three, however, are perfect replicas of the hormones secreted by animals, and for that matter by human beings.

The remaining two, Ralgro and Finaplix, are a synthetic tribute to man's ability to outdo nature. They are purely artificial concoctions of chemicals which work just like natural hormones . . . only more so. The two synthetic drugs tend to give better results than the so-called natural hormones, but the most dramatic performance is achieved when a combination of natural and synthetic is used. Therefore, in a determined effort to maximize profits, many farmers will give their cattle a 'cocktail' of two or three hormones.

Typically, a farmer will use Finaplix and Ralgro together in the last two months before slaughter. A year before he may have implanted Compudose, a long-lasting hormone. Or he may have started off with Compudose and then used either Finaplix or Synovex to finish off the fattening process. The possibilities are endless. And although most farmers realize they will get no extra benefit by using more than three implants, the drug companies admit there are still a few who believe that the more they pump in, the more they will get out. Moreover, beef cattle often move twice or three times to different types of farm for fattening, and each time they may be given a new implant by their new owner: all this goes to show just how widespread the use of hormones has become in Britain.

All five drugs have to be prescribed by a veterinary surgeon, though few have been known to raise objections. The beasts are injected by means of an ear implant, which may stay in place until the time of slaughter. Because ears should be cut off and thrown away by the abbatoir, the method is meant to reassure consumers that they are not eating huge doses of hormones.

The pharmaceutical industry is keen to point out that we have been experimenting with hormones for centuries. A hundred years ago the 'gelder' was a common sight travelling around the English countryside. For a penny a time he would castrate and spay the farm animals in the fields. His barbaric services were employed mainly for pigs and chickens, to fatten them up more quickly for market. But cattle might also receive his attentions – especially dairy cows, which would then never dry up. The spaying was done with a button hook, which was skilfully inserted through a slit in the animal's side to reach the uterus and ovaries. Once exposed, they could be neatly cut out. The results of these stomach-turning operations was to change the hormone balance in the animal. Since those early days, when it was discovered that a certain balance of male and female hormones would produce a fatter animal, farmers have been attempting to find the perfect formula.

In the more recent past hormones have been injected directly into the animal's rump, with dire consequences. In the late 'seventies, reports started to come in of a strange phenomenon amongst Italian children. Doctors found some 5–8-year-old girls and boys were developing sexually and they could not understand the cause. At the same time it was discovered that baby food contained a high level of the hormone diethylstilboestrol (DES), which had been used as a growth promoter on calves. The inevitable conclusion was drawn. The children must have been given this baby food at birth and it had speeded up the onset of puberty.

The hormone was also found in other meat products containing veal, though no more strange incidents were reported. It was thought to have come from one of the Iron Curtain countries, probably Czechoslovakia, injected into veal calves in France, which were then exported to Italy. And because the DES was injected, rather than implanted in the ear, huge residues of the drug were left in the meat.

Apart from being cited as the cause of a macabre early puberty, there is also strong evidence to link DES with cervical cancer. To allay fears, the EEC banned DES and all similar hormones, known as stilbenes, from use in all member countries in 1980.

Despite that early scare, at least half the meat we eat is still fattened artificially with hormones. Astonishing though this figure is, it is probably a conservative estimate. The farmers' governing body, the Meat and Livestock Commission, has admitted for the last two years that the problem is now this widespread. But in November 1985, when it gave evidence to a House of Lords select committee, it was clear that the Commission suspected the true percentage could be much higher. In answer to a question from Lord John-Mackie, Dr Allen, the Commission's Head of Beef Improvement Services, stated that the figure was now 'certainly in excess of 50 per cent and probably nearer 60 per cent'.

Whatever the true figure, hormones are currently big

business and are likely to remain so until the very day that the EEC ban takes effect. Farmers spend a total of over £5 million pounds a year on the drugs that will give them £21 million pounds' worth of extra meat to sell. A single beef animal can fetch up to £50 more at market if it has been implanted.

However, if the farming interests get their way, the ban may never become law. Already a huge campaign is under way to convince consumers that hormones can do no harm, and that the EEC's decision was a ludicrous pandering to public emotion. The animal drugs industry has produced brochures and leaflets explaining the benefits and giving the results of safety tests.

This literature emphasizes the 'naturalness' of the three 'natural' hormones and points out that eating unimplanted bull meat or old dairy cow meat would give us ten times more male or female hormones respectively than we would get from eating young cattle implanted with the same hormones. The writers even add up the hormones in a common cabbage in the hope of allaying our fears. A hundred grammes of cabbage has 2,400 nanograms of oestrogen, the female hormone, while a hundred grammes of steermeat implanted with the same manufactured version of oestrogen would give us only 11 ng of oestrogen.

While the cabbage argument cannot be faulted – surprisingly, plants contain the same hormones that the human body makes – it is likely to leave the British consumer unconvinced. No one likes the idea of additives in their food, except the producers and manufacturers, of course, who profit by their high-tech methods. But the question of growth promoters poses a tricky problem for health campaigners. The twist is that these worrying chemicals help to produce much leaner meat, an obvious bonus when so many people are trying to cut down on fat.

The effect is not just a small improvement. In trials, hormones have reduced the fat content of the carcass by 30 per cent. In one example, dairy cows which were being fattened for the slaughterhouse, using hormone implants, put on an extra 76 kilos in weight and almost half was lean meat.

The control group which was given no growth drugs had 12.8 kilos less lean. It is valuable lean too. Most of the extra meat appears on the rump to provide more steaks and high-quality roasting joints.

Away from the perfect conditions of the research stations, farmers themselves obtain similar, though not such extreme, results. On average hormone-treated cattle give 3 per cent extra lean at the expense of fat, which means a normal steer or heifer would produce about 18 more useful pounds of lean meat.

Hormones also have the effect of decreasing the amount of fat within the cuts so that fatty pockets within joints are smaller and the marbling less obvious. With about two-thirds of our meat animals now being artificially fattened, that means a lot less heart-stopping fat on our plates.

To the butcher the proportion of lean meat on the carcass is now vital. Customers are starting to demand well-trimmed meat but do not want to pay a higher price for it. Farmers have saved the butcher's bacon by producing the extra kilos of top-value lean meat, at little extra cost.

The five hormones left in use as growth promoters all work in a very different way from the stilbenes. They are not directly injected into the body of the animal. If we eat small amounts of these hormones they just pass straight through: the body does not have the ability to absorb them. (This is not true of the stilbenes.)

This is why all the scientific studies have shown that the hormones currently used to fatten cattle are highly unlikely to have any effect on us at all. But the European Parliament, in its wisdom, decided that our opinions should outweigh the views of scientists on the hormone question.

After many years of debate the Agricultural Council of the EEC decided hormones should not be used on any meat animals after 1 January 1988, though Britain had a 'stay of execution' until 1989. Although this crucial decision was supposedly made to protect our health, the very committee which had been specially set up to report on the dangers of hormones, if any, never got the chance to present its evidence.

It was chaired by an Englishman, Professor Eric Lamming, who views the events in the latter part of 1985 with amazement. In his opinion, his committee was gagged.

The European Parliament voted overwhelmingly for a ban on all hormones on 11 October. The decision was a political one, based on the enormous consumer pressure that had built up against the drugs. There was also an 800,000-tonne mountain of frozen beef to consider. Many MEPs felt that they could not condone the use of drugs to boost meat production if the surplus was only going to be stored away in costly refrigeration plants. But the vote to outlaw hormones meant that the body of worthy scientists who had been beavering away for four years had suddenly become an embarrassment. They were due to publish their long-awaited report at the end of the year, and the rumours suggested they would give all the products on the market a clean bill of health.

If they were allowed to report, how could the EEC justify a total ban? The problem was solved quite simply. On 26 October the scientific committee was suspended by the Agricultural Commissioner, four days before it was due to meet to complete the final draft. That left the way clear for the Agricultural Council to agree with the decision for a ban at its meeting on 20 December.

The suspension order arrived on Professor Lamming's desk by telex, and caused private fury amongst his committee members around Europe. As a result, their expert view – that hormones currently used were not likely to endanger health – was never publicly heard.

The Professor sees the events as a terrible indictment of the EEC decision-making system. In the UK, ministries may disagree with the views of their expert committees; they may try to influence them; they may attempt to tone down their conclusions; but they could never prevent them from producing a report. While the consumer view undoubtedly won the day in Brussels, it may be that the strange proceedings which have brought charges of a 'cover-up' from the pharmaceutical industry will force the issue to be re-examined, and allow the farmers to get their way. Already the British government has appealed to the European Court to give its opinion on the decision to ban hormones, and at the time of going to press its view was still awaited.

Whatever the eventual outcome, it is unlikely that the British public will ever be happy about eating meat that has been injected with hormones. They are, quite understandably, an emotive subject. Hormones affect us in strange ways. Even small changes in hormonal levels can make women weepy, or aggressive, before a period. They can make teenagers hell to live with and they can make anyone energetic or lethargic. Most people have suffered from the effects of hormones in some way or another. Even if a thousand scientific studies showed that they could do us no harm, most of us would still prefer not to take a chance. Consumers have a long memory. They remember the Thalidomide, and Opren disasters: both these drugs had passed the safety tests and been licensed by expert committees. Less tragic, but still of vital concern to many mothers, are the effects of colourings, flavourings and preservatives, especially on children.

This heightened public awareness of additives has developed a new trend amongst today's shoppers to avoid any chemicals in food which are not absolutely necessary. As a result, firms have already sprung up which are willing to cater for shoppers who prefer to eat 'uncontaminated' meat. Carol Hockey's Newtown Farm in Fordingbridge, Hants., supplies additive-free meat to individual customers all over Britain using the British Rail Red Star service. The wholesaler Canvin International of Bedford was doubling its output each week during the spring of 1985 as more and more beef farmers joined their additive-free scheme. Butchers reported an enthusiastic response to the meat which carried a 'no chemicals' sticker. But an even more heartwarming success story is to be found in Wiltshire, where a newly married farming couple have spread their ideas on the right way to raise stock to dozens of farms in the south. Calling themselves the Real Meat Company, they have found that the idea of animals kept humanely and given no unnecessary chemicals has struck a sympathetic chord with customers all over the West Country. By July 1986, just six months after starting the whole scheme, they had opened their first retail butcher's shop in Bath selling only their version of 'real meat'.

2

Medication gone mad

Ironically, the EEC ban on hormones did not mention the widespread use of antibiotics, though there is far more evidence that they could pose a threat to our health than there has ever been against hormones. For while the hormones industry would seem to have no future, the antibiotics business is booming. Farmers are buying £20 million worth of these drugs a year, and the market is expanding rapidly. There is evidence that antibiotics make up almost two-thirds of all animal medicines administered, while in human medicine the figure is only one-third.

The drugs are no longer used solely to treat infection, but are being given to animals who are not sick simply to ward off the possibility of infection, and in some cases they are used blatantly as growth-promoters. This area of the 'pharming' business is potentially one of the most dangerous so far uncovered. Not only are some people allergic to antibiotic residues which may be left in the meat, but routine dosing could lead to lethal bacteria developing a resistance to drugs used in human medicine. With only a limited number of antibiotics available to them, doctors could be faced with an epidemic for which they have no antidote.

The biggest threat is likely to come from salmonella and other intestinal bacteria, although a 1983 report by the Food Advisory Committee in Eire warned of many other serious illnesses which could be left with no cure: 'Organisms so far known to be involved include the causative agents of such diseases as typhoid fever, infantile gastro-enteritis, pyelitis, plague and cholera.'

Because ailments in animals have always been treated with the same antibiotics as those developed for man, any resistance built up in animals poses a serious problem for human medicine. Drugs such as penicillin, ampecillin, chloramphenicol, the tetracyclines and the sulphonamides are just as popular in the cowshed as they are on the hospital ward.

Some bacteria easily become resistant to a certain drug if it is used against them regularly. New strains develop, called phages, which can repel the drug the next time it is used. Moreover, these resistant bugs can pass on their resistant ability – the R factor – to other bugs with which they come into contact. They do not even have to belong to the same bug family, and it is possible that they may pass on the know-how to resist many different antibiotics of the same general family.

While the bacteria remain in the animal's gut there is no problem. But as the animal passes through the slaughterhouse its meat can be quickly contaminated by bacteria from the discarded intestines. Some may be resistant, and may then take up residence in our stomachs if we eat the meat. Only thorough cooking will destroy all the bugs that may be present.

What happens then if they multiply to such an extent that we fall seriously ill? The doctors will reach for an antibiotic and could find it has no effect. With some conditions, such as typhoid and dysentery, the medical men have few choices. The R factor could then prove fatal.

Many of the antibiotics available on prescription are precisely the same drugs that we use on ourselves. The best-known, penicillin, is used to treat numerous infections on the farm, from abscesses on calves to meningitis in piglets. Most of us have good reason to know how vital it is in human medicine, for all manner of infections. Doctors often depend on it to treat serious illnesses – including pneumonia, meningitis and syphilis.

Ampecillin – penicillin's synthetic form – is just as popular for a wide variety of animal infections. In humans it can be a vital drug when the cause of infection is not known. Many of us will have had ampecillin from the dentist to treat an abscess under the tooth; it is also used in the treatment of cystitis.

Like penicillin, the tetracyclines were developed early and immediately went into service for both man and animals. Doctors look to them to cure infections in the stomach or intestine, but particularly to treat virus ailments such as typhoid and venereal disease. Farmers use them to relieve calves with 'transit fever' – a type of pneumonia brought on by long and uncomfortable journeys to and from market.

The various drugs in the sulphonamide family are widely used in poultry production to prevent serious diseases such as coccidiosis, and in man they may be used wherever penicillin would normally be used, and can therefore be especially valuable where the patient has an allergy to the various drugs in the penicillin family.

Probably the most dangerous veterinary antibiotic of all is chloramphenicol. Farm vets still prescribe it for pneumonia in young animals, serious stomach problems and even eye infections. But in human medicine it is a vital last resort for many fatal illnesses, including typhoid.

One variation of the salmonella bug is giving the scientists cause for concern already. At a conference of the British Veterinary Association in 1984 microbiologists likened it to 'the contents of a witch's cauldron'. The bug, called *S. typhimurium*, is the most common cause of salmonella food poisoning, but is particularly adept at developing resistance.

'New phage types are continually emerging, each one with a bigger and better antibiotic resistance pattern,' the BVA reported. 'At present none of these phage types is particularly dangerous to man. This is fortunate because if it were to acquire added virulence for man we might be faced with an epidemic in food animals of a disease with the same potential for human illness as typhoid.'

It is probably no coincidence that food poisoning due to this bug has been rising at an alarming rate in the last few years. The figure for 1983 showed that cases had increased by 28 per cent in just one year. Levels of other forms of infection are also on the increase. In England and Wales food poisoning increased by 20 per cent each year for the three years up to 1983. In that year over 15,000 serious cases were notified to the authorities, not to mention the instances that were never officially reported. More than two-thirds of the reported cases were caused by meat or meat products.

Food poisoning can be fatal, especially if for any reason the patient does not respond to drugs. Twenty-five people are known to have died in 1983 because of a salmonella infection. Eighteen of the deaths were caused by the *S. typhimurium* bacteria.

This surprising rate of increase is all the more disturbing in an age when science should be helping to reduce disease. Environmental health officers, who are responsible for checking the hygiene of factories, restaurants and shops, feel they are fighting a losing battle. Despite wide public understanding of food health hazards, and numerous prosecutions each year against unhygienic establishments, the food poisoning outbreaks get worse.

Many of us are unaware that we are harbouring resistant bacteria within our bodies. Research shows that 25–50 per cent of perfectly healthy adults and children are carriers of resistant bacteria. In small numbers they can do us no harm. It is only when they multiply and make us ill that we become vulnerable. They may have become resistant because we have undertaken a course of antibiotics. But many experts now believe a large proportion of the resistant bugs have arrived with us from the meat we have eaten.

Their conclusions are supported by the vast increase in resistant bacteria found in our bodies. Evidence from a number of reports from different countries was compiled by Eire's Food Advisory Committee and showed an alarming rise.

In 1962 only 3 per cent of the population had any resistant *S. typhimurium* bacteria. By 1982 52 per cent of us produced resistant *S. typhimurium*. The story was the same with the *E. coli* bug which is familiar to anyone who has suffered with 'gippy tummy'. In 1962 10 per cent of us had resistant bugs. By 1982 the figure had risen to 66 per cent.

More worrying is the dramatic rise in the degree of resistance found in *Staphylococcus aureus*, which causes abscesses. In 1962 42 per cent of us displayed evidence that we had resistant bugs, but twenty years later 80 per cent of us had bacteria which would not respond to certain antibiotics.

'Studies have separately demonstrated the common identity of resistant strains from calves, and persons consuming their meat, and from meat and food products and their consumers,' said the Food Committee's report.

British research on resistant bacteria in animals shows that the problem is not limited to calves. All cattle and pigs are playing host to bugs which are developing resistance. Some bugs are getting particularly clever at resisting certain antibiotics. A study by Sojka, Wray and McLaren published in the *British Veterinary Journal* shows that in just three years between 1979 and 1981 some bugs have become amazingly resistant to particular antibiotics. In pigs, for example, that busy little bug the *S. typhimurium* is now ten times more likely to resist chlortetracycline, one of the main tetracycline drugs. In 1979 5 per cent of *S. typhimurium* were resistant. By 1981 52 per cent failed to respond to this important drug.

The bacteria in pigs also show a rapid rise in resistance to chloramphenicol and ampecillin. The story is similar for cattle, in which bacteria are particularly good at ignoring the effects of the sulphonamide drugs and the tetracylines. In 1981 a staggering 93 per cent of *S. typhimurium* were resistant to sulphonamides.

These resistance problems were predicted as long ago as 1968 by a government committee headed by Professor Michael Swann. It concluded that the unnecessary use of antibiotics which are also used to treat man could lead to 'a potentially explosive situation'. The committee argued: 'It is clearly undesirable that situations should be allowed to arise in which the treatment of human illness would be limited because of antibiotic resistance in the causal organism or that highly pathogenic organisms, such as *Salmonella typhimurium*, should acquire resistance to antibiotics.'

The Swann report urged strongly that human antibiotics should not be used without a vet's prescription for the routine dosing of meat animals. As a result, today's over-the-counter growth-promotion products are licensed only if it can be shown that the antibiotic used is not suitable for human medication. However, there is still a possibility that some of them may leave residues in the meat which might just be harmful.

This type of growth promoter comes in the form of a medicated feed. Small amounts of antimicrobial are added to compound feeds, often by the manufacturer, and are used routinely by the farmer for raising calves, pigs and poultry. They need no prescription and are often used as the final ingredient in a cocktail of hormonal growth promoters. These drug supplements have become so popular in the last few years that it is now difficult to find a bag of feed that does not have them added.

The drugs work in two ways. Either they kill off some of the parasitic bacteria in the animal's gut in order to help it make better use of its digested food. Or they limit the numbers of bacteria and encourage the drug to help in the animal's digestion. The bug 'controllers' give us even less to worry about than the 'killers' since they can leave no residue in the meat. Neither can be shown to develop any kind of resistant bacteria which could affect man.

No one can ever be certain, but in the light of our current medical knowledge it is unlikely that the growth-promoters will ever become a serious health risk. The public outcry over growth promoting medicated feeds has been misdirected, for it is the use of prescription drugs that should be giving cause for concern.

Apart from growth promotion, there are two other reasons for using antibiotics on the farm – though the dividing line between them is considerably blurred. The most obvious use is therapeutic. Clearly, when an animal is ill, a shot of antibiotic is necessary to put it on its feet again. This can only be done with a vet's prescription, and the same vet will oversee the animal's recovery. But the medical profession is worried – not about the necessary one-off doses of drugs given to a sick animal, but about the regular dosing of other animals who may not even be sick. Bacteria are only likely to build up resistance to certain drugs if they are given over a period of time.

The grey area occurs when farmers give their animals a prophylactic dose of drugs: in other words, they try to prevent disease before it has started. It is common in a pig or calf unit, say, to treat every animal in the same building with antibiotics if just one is sick. In this way the farmer can protect his investment, and ward off what could be a financial disaster. As an added bonus, the antibiotics will also work wonders at promoting extra-fast growth in the stock.

'The prophylactic use is the most worrying at the moment,' says Gordon Applebe, head of the law department of the Pharmaceutical Society. 'It may be preventing disease, but it is also acting as a growth promoter and it is now very widespread. The drugs involved are often the same drugs used for man and so you have the problem of a resistance build-up. The trouble is, if you're rearing poultry, veal or pigs on a battery system and one animal gets sick, then you could lose the lot overnight if you don't prescribe a prophylactic dose of antibiotic.'

Vets are aware of the economic pressures on the farmer, and will rarely refuse to prescribe drugs for animals in that situation. But according to Professor Alan Linton of Bristol University Medical School, not all the prophylactic uses are justified.

'The vet is supposed to use his training and skill to decide when antibiotics are needed. But it has to be said – a lot of them are being used unnecessarily. This is indiscriminate therapy and it is dangerous,' he says.

The difference between a therapeutic dose, given to a sick animal, and a prophylactic dose, given to ward off disease, is simply one of amount. And though the preventative dose is less than the therapeutic, it is far more than the amount of antibiotic that goes into the growth-promoting products. Since higher doses breed greater resistance in bacteria, large-scale preventative medicine in our meat industry is not to be encouraged.

It is factory-farming methods that have led farmers to seek

31

ways of insuring against outbreaks of disease. When animals were bred and raised in open fields sick individuals could be more easily isolated, and bacteria found it more difficult to spread. According to the government's Agricultural Development and Advisory Service, the trend for raising stock in indoor units has led to a steady increase in disease.

'Calf losses have increased since 1958 and reached a peak in 1969, from which they have since declined,' said a 1984 ADAS report on the cattle industry. 'The increase coincided with the development of intensive calf units and the move towards loose housing of cows, both of which increased the chances of cross-infection.'

One of the reasons why diseases have been kept at bay since 1969 is the wide use of antibiotics. But some vets and doctors feel it is wrong to be using vital drugs to prop up bad farm management. They argue that different housing, more ventilation and more common sense from the farmer could prevent much of the disease.

'The real problem is intensive rearing,' says Professor Linton. 'The farmer wants to get away with the cheapest possible methods that he can, so the structure, hygiene and ventilation of the buildings is poor. The animals are kept in close proximity to each other so when you have an outbreak in one animal the vet is forced to treat the lot. In that situation there will be far greater use of an antibiotic than you'd expect in human medicine. You wouldn't treat every member of the family living in the same house with a drug if only one was infected. In my opinion some vets and farmers are ignorant of the consequences,' he says.

Our system of rearing stock, which involves shunting the animals vast distances around the country, is also responsible for much of the unnecessary use of drugs. Methods are now so intensive that farmers often specialize in raising animals only for a certain period of their lives. So, in beef production for example, a dairy farmer will do the breeding, another will raise the calves until they are about a year old, and yet another will 'finish' them ready for slaughter. In addition, some farms deal only in heifers, others in steers. Much the same system operates for pigs, and even some lambs are moved about when they are sent to fattening farms.

The result of this concentration of effort is that small groups of young animals have to travel long distances to new homes. Many will have been bought and sold at the local market. When they arrive at their new home they will invariably be mixed in with many other young animals from different sources, since the farmer's aim is to have groups of exactly the same age.

This system is a recipe for trouble. Just as humans are more susceptible to bugs in a foreign country, so animals are more likely to pick up diseases when they have spent time in a crowded market and are then mixed in with strangers.

'A lot of our animal husbandry practices involve moving calves up to 100 miles because a farmer wants to gather, say, 40 animals of the same age on the same date,' says Professor Linton. 'The result is that they're exposed to stress and shock. When they arrive at the rearing farm they may not have had foot or water and can often be very sick animals. They may need to be given antibiotics simply to keep them alive.

'In my opinion this is a misuse of these important drugs. We are using them to prop up bad animal husbandry, and we are doing it over and over again.'

The Swann report made it clear that any antibiotic given for purposes other than growth promotion must be prescribed by the vet who has the animals under his care. But this direction is being ignored by many farmers who have found a way to get round the rules. Because many vets are concerned about resistance problems, there are some circumstances in which they are likely to refuse antibiotics for the prevention of disease. The desire to give calves regular prophylactic dosing is one of them. Aware of this reluctance, feed manufacturers have been offering farmers a prescription written out by their own in-house vet. This enables the farmer to take delivery of calf feed with a ready-prepared dose of antibiotic in the mix. Sometimes it has been added without the authority of a vet's prescription.

Many local vets are unaware that their farmers are making

use of this service, including a vet from the West Country who told of his experience.

'One of my farmers, who rears calves, asked me to prescribe a course of antibiotics for some calves that were due to arrive from market in a few days' time. I told him I couldn't do that. I could only prescribe for them if they were actually sick, and we wouldn't know that until they arrived. He seemed satisfied with that answer, but when I did my next visit I was in for a shock.

'The calves had arrived the day before and, indeed, they were suffering badly from transit sickness, so I was prepared to write out a prescription. Then I discovered the calves were already being given antibiotics with their feed. It had been already mixed by the manufacturer, and I was expected to provide the prescription to make the whole thing legal.

'This seems to be becoming normal practice, and while I think most market calves do need antibiotics, I am very worried to think that feed suppliers are taking the vet's responsibility upon themselves.'

If the indiscriminate use of antibiotics is to be controlled, then this glaring loophole must be closed. Many veterinary experts feel that it should be illegal for a vet in the employ of one of the feed or drug companies to be able to prescribe his paymaster's products. As yet the Ministry of Agriculture has not acknowledged that this problem exists, much less done anything to curb it.

Even if we rely solely on the local vet to protect the interests of human health, he may still be subject to awkward pressures. One major farmer in the vet's area may contribute a substantial amount to his income, which would make it difficult to refuse his requests.

'Some vets are more browbeaten than others,' says Gordon Applebe. 'But most don't like the thought of losing a large client. It may mean they will be more flexible when it comes to prescribing preventative drugs.'

Pressure from the feed merchants can also make life difficult for the small local vet. 'They are often big businesses who use experts with fancy titles to go round visiting farms and offering advice,' says Mr Applebe. 'They may persuade the farmer he can't do without some sort of antibiotic feed and he'll then expect his vet to prescribe it. If the vet refuses he's then up against the massed expertise and knowledge of these consultants.'

Doctors are also concerned that some antibiotics may leave traces in the meat which could cause allergic reactions in sensitive people. In Britain we do no routine checks for residues at slaughterhouses, and so meat badly contaminated from antibiotics, hormones or any other drugs could easily find its way into the shops.

Between August and November of 1982 vets at four slaughterhouses in Dublin checked the kidneys from carcasses to discover how great a threat this might be. They found an astonishing 45 per cent of pigs had anti-bacterial residues in their meat. The figure for cattle was 7.7 per cent, and was exactly the same for sheep.

'It is considered that these residues most likely arose either as a result of the administration of chemotherapeutical substances to the animals during the last week or so of their life, or, in the case of pigs, of a failure on the part of the producer to withhold antibiotic-medicated feedstuffs during the ten days or so prior to slaughter,' said their report.

The only checks carried out in Britain for residues are done by the Ministry of Agriculture at various laboratories. Compared to the situation in most European countries only a tiny fraction of animals are checked for residues of drugs, the collation of data is vague and the figures are unbelievably low. According to the Ministry it is not possible for figures to be provided year by year, but we must make do with the knowledge that one per cent of meat tested between 1981 and 1983 showed levels of antibiotic, and during 1983 and 1984 the figure was .5 per cent.

The surprisingly low statistics may be due to the fact that the tests done by the Ministry are not particularly good at picking up low levels of some hormones and antibiotics. More sensitive tests were being developed at the Institute of Animal Research in Newbury, but in the spring of 1986 the Ministry

35

phased out its research programme. Workers at the Institute were furious that their efforts had been in vain, and some were privately suspicious that the Ministry had deliberately prevented the development of more sensitive tests in order to protect the drugs and farming industries.

Our main protection from residues lies in the withdrawal times stipulated for all prescribed antibiotics, and for the two synthetic hormones. In order to get their licence, their manufacturers must suggest a period of time during which the farmer must wait after giving the animals the drug and before sending them for slaughter. The Veterinary Products Committee of the Ministry of Agriculture then checks that the suggested withdrawal time is adequate and, if it is happy, grants the licence. As long as vets oversee the use of drugs, then these withdrawal times are likely to be kept, and the meat should be uncontaminated.

Residue problems are thought to arise when the vet writes the prescription but leaves the farmer to administer the drug. Many therapeutic and prophylactic antibiotics are given in water and feedstuffs rather than by injection. Then the vet cannot oversee the dosing, and when clearing an animal for the slaughterhouse may not know it has recently received some sort of drug.

Not all antibiotics have the ability to pass into the meat of an animal, but those that do can make life very uncomfortable for people who suffer allergic reactions. It takes only a minute dose of an allergen to produce a response in some sufferers, and the more often that allergy is triggered, the worse their body's response can become. Luckily most people come into contact with antibiotics only occasionally in their lives. If they are allergic it is usually a simple matter for the doctor to change to a different drug next time one is needed. But the constant nagging of antibiotic residues from meat on a hypersensitive person can turn a minor discomfort into a major health problem.

'Many hypersensitivity reactions manifest themselves as relatively benign, albeit uncomfortable, rashes,' says the Dublin Food Committee's report. 'However with repeated exposure, and often even on first exposure, much more serious reactions may develop, including urticaria, anaphylactic shock, serum sickness, arthropathy, lymphadenopathy, nephropathy, gastro-enteritis, encephalitis, hepatitis, and anaemia. Fatalities can occur.'

There is little evidence in Britain that a large number of people with allergies are the victims of antibiotic residues in food. Such a link is very difficult to trace without extensive medical tests. But we do know that the opposite link is true – that certain antibiotics have a high likelihood of causing an allergy. For example, the sulphonamide group of drugs, which is used extensively for poultry, is likely to cause allergic reactions in 13 per cent of the population. About 11 per cent of us are allergic to the penicillins, including ampecillin.

If the regular eating of meat residues has caused someone to have an allergic reaction to an antibiotic, another, possibly more disturbing, possibility will arise. In the event of a serious illness the range of antibiotics at the doctor's disposal may be limited. If the bacteria causing the illness are also resistant to some drugs, the situation could prove highly dangerous.

It is not just the legal supply of animal drugs that puts our health at risk. Behind the cowsheds a thriving trade in black-market drugs exists. Although British rules on animal medicines are some of the most relaxed in Europe, there are still a few profit-hungry farmers who buy even more than their legal allowance of drugs by resorting to under-the-counter sales.

Investigators from the Pharmaceutical Society recently exposed a huge animal drugs ring operating in the West Country. In a £30,000 racket, a Wiltshire agricultural merchant was supplying medicines illegally to local farmers from his home in Devizes. The drugs, in this case, were all antibiotics which can be given lawfully only with a vet's prescription. But the merchant had discovered a chain of supply from the manufacturers which meant his customers could dispense with the services of their vet. It was the perfect system. The drugs were far cheaper since the farmer could administer them himself and thus save the vet's call-out charge. Of course, there was no VAT to pay either. And with such a huge potential market, the crooked dealer needed a much smaller profit margin on the sale of the drugs than a vet would have charged. But the most worrying advantage gained by the farmers involved was the total lack of any supervision over withdrawal times.

For most antibiotics and the two synthetic hormones there are legal limitations on how soon any animal which has been given a drug may be slaughtered after ceasing to take the drug. They vary from a few days to three months and are meant to protect our health. Before animals may be sent for slaughter the farm vet has to certify that none is still affected by any drug. But with medicines bought on the black market and administered by the farmer himself, the vet can have no way of knowing that the animals he is sending to slaughter could be a danger to human health.

Devizes magistrates court heard five specimen charges: that the merchant had, on three occasions, illegally supplied prescription-only medicines to farmers, and that on two occasions he had unlawfully made supplies to other merchants. But the scale of his activities was so large that when he faced the bench in October 1985 he asked for no less than 254 other cases to be taken into consideration!

The West Country ring is by no means an isolated example. The sleuths from the Pharmaceutical Society believe they have uncovered merely the tip of the iceberg. The Devizes dealer was at the end of a complicated supply network for illegal drugs which could extend all over Britain. Although he was only dealing in antibiotics, it is likely that drug rings are also supplying hormones illegally. The banned DES could be made by any amateur in a garden shed, and supplied to any farmers willing to stop at nothing to gain extra profits. Already evidence has been gathered in other countries which could lead to more court cases. In Scotland dealers have been brought to justice for illegally importing hormones from Eire, where they are much cheaper.

Using black-market drugs can bring complications of a different kind. Because the hand wielding the hypodermic is an amateur's, the farmer's, he may not always take the same professional care. A London cabdriver discovered the possible consequences in March 1985 when he bit into a needle tip in his continental sausage. The result was a badly gashed mouth and £340 worth of repair work to his teeth and gums. Because the tip did not contain any curing solution it was highly unlikely that it had been left in the meat at the processing stage. The most likely explanation was that it had been used to inject a living animal. And since any vet worth his salt would notice if he broke his hypodermic, the chances are that the injection was given by an amateur.

No one can say with any certainty how many farmers are using under-the-counter medicines at present, but they could be adding up to 10 per cent more artificially fattened meat to the market than is known about officially. That means it is possible that seven out of ten pork chops, for example, may have been produced with the help of chemicals.

When the EEC ban takes effect in 1989, the drug companies warn that this black market could grow considerably. They fear that farmers who know the benefits hormones can bring will be tempted to make use of illicit sources which are bound to multiply. Dealers might make their own drugs, bring them in from non-EEC countries, or even find a way to tap the legal supply of other hormonal products.

For even though growth-promoting hormones will be banned, therapeutic hormones will still be supplied. At the moment the Ministry of Agriculture licenses seven hormones for the treatment of sick animals, most of them for fertility problems. In the wrong hands some of these may also prove useful for growth promotion.

Hormones and antibiotics are not the only drugs known to help fatten our animals. Intensive systems may depend on tranquillizers to obtain the best possible weight gain. As in humans, stress can cause animals to burn up energy and so prevent them getting fat. Overcrowding, indoor housing and boredom all contribute to the build-up of stress, especially in pigs and cattle. /

To the farmer, this means he is not getting the full benefit from the carefully planned daily rations fed to his stock. Rather than change the system, some rearers are turning to tranquillizers to keep their animals 'content'. Given in small doses they will counteract the stressful conditions and allow the animals to put on weight as if they are living freely, in the open air.

Pigs are particularly susceptible to stress, and it is common to use drugs to keep them calm. Because they have a nasty habit of attacking strangers, when a new batch arrives in a pig unit *all* the inhabitants may be dosed with tranquillizers in order to prevent fights.

Sows often need to be kept docile with drugs, too, especially if they are kept in the barbaric 'tether' system. Although pigs have a similar intelligence to dogs, some farmers chain them up tightly in stalls so that they spend the whole of their lives standing in the same position. This is done solely for the convenience of cheap and easy maintenance, but the sow often displays her frustration by banging the sides of her stall and injuring herself. Removing the chains would be expensive; an injection is the easy option.

Tranquillizing drugs are also widely used to keep animals quiet on long journeys. In many cases this is to the animal's benefit, since in its fear it may do a lot of harm both to itself and its companions. But concern has been expressed about the possibility of residues of these drugs getting into the meat, especially if the animals were injected before their trip to the slaughterhouse.

Tranquillizers are available only on a vet's prescription, but some have no set withdrawal time which would prevent their use on the day of slaughter. This is not necessarily because a withdrawal limit is not needed. Some of these drugs have been on the market for years and have never had to go through the approval system of the Veterinary Products Committee, which lays down safe withdrawal periods. Because they were in existence before the Committee, some tranquillizers have a licence 'as of right', and so there are no rules that would prevent them being used just before slaughter.

The EEC has urged that all member countries make sure their veterinary products are approved by a safety committee, but the time limit for putting this into effect does not run out until 1991. Until all drugs have been scrutinized, we rely on the common sense of the vet not to prescribe them if there is any chance they might taint our meat.

The facts prove that the indiscriminate handing out of drugs to farm animals cannot be allowed to continue. Vets must be given every support to stand up to the might of big landowners and commercial feed companies. In-house vets must be banned from prescribing their own products. And farmers must be made more aware of the crucial importance of not putting profit before human health.

Animal pharm of the future

The latest drugs to be used on the farm could mean spring-time will never be quite the same again. Rather than the pleasing sight of a lamb gambolling by the side of its mother, in future we could think we are seeing double . . . or triple. Birth drugs are about to be used which could mean ewes will have three, four or five lambs at their sides.

Ovulation stimulants have been devised which will push up the lambing average. At present, ewes will produce either one lamb or two. Triplets are still a rarity. But the new drugs could mean three lambs will become the norm, and thus make sheep-rearing more profitable.

The drugs are being given to the ewe before ovulation to stimulate her ovaries to produce more eggs. Fertilization is timed carefully to ensure the best possible response, and so far the researchers have had a great deal of success.

The drugs are now available commercially and in the spring of 1986 a number of farmers tried them. But there are still problems to be ironed out. When triplets arrive naturally, one of the three lambs is usually given to a ewe who has either lost her offspring or only has one to cope with. But since most treated ewes produce three or four lambs there are not enough 'spare' mothers to go round. The ewes have to raise their extra-large family themselves and the researchers do not yet know how that will affect their health in the long run.

Even more futuristic is the possibility that genetic engineering will find a place down on the farm. In 1982 scientists made a breakthrough by mixing the genes from rats and mice to produce a giant mouse. They isolated the gene responsible for a rat's growth and fused it with the fertilized egg from a mouse to produce a Frankensteinian result.

The implications for meat production in the twenty-first century are tremendous. In theory it may be possible to mix the growth potential of a buffalo, say, with the embryo of a calf, to produce an animal that is nothing more than a huge meat machine. The question is, how would we ever fit the T-bone steak on our plate?

3

Animal rites . . . and wrongs

When we buy our meat, most of us prefer not to think about how the animal met its end. We know that slaughterhouses are not pleasant places, but if we choose to eat meat, then we accept that animals must be killed. But when the knife falls, all of us trust that it is done in the most humane manner possible. We do not want those creatures killed to provide our food to suffer any unnecessary pain or cruelty. And we rest our faith in the government and its officials to ensure that our obligation as human beings is kept. If you are a meat-eater, is that a fair summary of your feelings?

If so, how appalled will you be to discover that in two important respects the government gives its backing to practices which have been condemned as inhumane, and that you and I eat meat regularly which comes from these sources. The first of these has attracted a tangle of justifications and denials of suffering, yet much scientific evidence points to its cruelty. The second is all the more objectionable because it is entirely without justification, and causes the animal unnecessary distress during the crucial last moments of its life.

The two practices relate to religious slaughter and live tenderization. Both have been condemned by the government-appointed Farm Animal Welfare Council, yet the Minister of Agriculture has done nothing to stop the misery. Not only that, he has not even made it possible for consumers to prevent the suffering by boycotting meat produced in these ways. In neither case does this meat have to be identified in the shop. So whatever we think of the morality of the methods, we cannot vote with our purses.

Most people are probably aware that there are problems with the way we slaughter our food animals. Undoubtedly some arrive at the slaughterhouse bruised and suffering from a long journey; some are fearful when they approach their end; and some fail to be knocked unconscious before the slaughterman's knife does its job. While these cruelties are enough to cause us great concern, they are already covered by the law. If the slaughterhouse staff mistreat an animal when it is unloaded, or waiting its turn, they are committing an offence. If they allow a creature to see one of its fellows being killed, that again is an offence. And if the system is not good enough to make sure that every animal is either killed instantaneously, or stunned into unconscious oblivion before its life is ended, then again the slaughterhouse can be prosecuted. It is the duty of the local authority inspectors, and the vets in attendance, to make sure that these laws are kept.

However, if a slaughterhouse kills by cutting an animal's throat while it is fully conscious, or gives a tenderizing injection while it is still alive, there is nothing the law can do. Both acts are quite legal in Britain. They have escaped the scrutiny of the law because they are shrouded in mystery. In the first case, religious tradition is held to be above the understanding of outsiders. And in the second, the company which patented the tenderizing technique prefers to keep very quiet about its operations.

Yet it is only by understanding what happens to some of our meat animals that we can make up our minds to change things. While the public appears not to care the government will not tackle such 'hot potatoes'. To make a realistic assessment of the morality of these practices you need to know something about how a slaughterhouse operates. So that's where we'll start.

Making a killing

Each year 480 million poultry and 34 million cattle, calves, sheep and pigs arrive at the slaughterhouse either direct from the farm or from the livestock market. Most farmers care enough about their stock to see that they are properly loaded and cannot come to any harm on the journey. But when animals come from market they may well be tired, hungry, thirsty and bewildered. Unloading is often the first distressing experience for them. The law says ramps must be at the right height and must not lead on to slippery surfaces, but there are still accidents, especially with animals who have suffered on the journey.

At the plant they must be rested, fed and watered in comfortable surroundings. This means that horned bullocks, for instance, if they are fractious, should be separated, and that any creatures who have suffered injury during their time in the lorry should be put out of their misery by emergency slaughter. Animals may stay in this waiting area for just a few hours or overnight until they have settled down.

Most of us find it difficult to accept that any animal would settle in these circumstances. We tend to believe that they would scent danger and would be fearful of their fate. But this does not appear to be the case. Many scientific studies have shown that despite their close proximity to death, all biological signs of fear are absent in animals that are well treated. Their heart beat, blood pressure and nervous activity are normal both in the waiting area and en route to the slaughter room.

This last walk is known as the 'race', and in most designs it will be curved so that the animal's natural inquisitiveness will lead it along the path. Most follow the route willingly. Occasionally the handlers resort to a prod – sometimes from a stick, more often from an electric goad.

The law says food animals should not see their fellows killed, and that death should be painless – though there are exceptions, which will be explained later. The slaughterhouse should either use a method which is instantaneous or stun the animal into unconsciousness so that it is unaware of the fatal blow. For this reason cattle are driven into a 'stunning pen', a box which can be closed in to fit the size of the animal, so that it cannot kick or struggle. Immediately, it will be shot through the brain with a special, retractable bolt. Surprising as this may seem, the bolt does not kill, but certainly removes the animal to an oblivion from which it never recovers. The side of the stunning pen is lowered and the body rolls to the floor. Cattle, calves and some sheep are stunned in this way. Other sheep, pigs and goats will be given an electric shock through the temples to knock them out. Occasionally, pigs are stunned in a special gas chamber, though this alternative is more expensive than the other methods.

The unconscious bodies will be hoisted by a hind leg on to a moving conveyor, and there, hanging by a leg, the main blood vessels just above the heart will be stuck (stabbed) so that the creature bleeds to death. Why such a bloody end? Many of us do not realize what to the butcher is obvious. Since the carcass must be hung for up to three weeks, any blood remaining in the veins and arteries is a source of disease. The meat would be a danger to health. It has always been thought that the only efficient way to drain the carcass of blood is with the help of a beating heart, though recent research suggests that the same amount of blood will leave the carcass whether the heart is beating or not. But slaughterhouses remain to be convinced and most animals' lives must ebb away as the blood flows from their bodies. Because the majority of us cannot accept that it would be right to bleed an animal to death while fully conscious, we have laws which demand pre-stunning. But Jews and Muslims are exempt from those rules and this is what has caused the passionate argument between the pro- and anti-religious slaughter lobbies.

Rites of slaughter

Ritual slaughter, as it is often termed, is based on deep-rooted beliefs which are fundamental to the faiths of those who practise it. It cannot be criticized lightly. Nor must it be used as part of any racist argument. But not surprisingly, the question of ritual slaughter arouses passionate views on both sides.

What exactly is it? Well, put simply, religious slaughter as practised in this country involves slitting the animal's throat with an exceedingly sharp knife, when it is fully conscious.

Both Jews and most Muslims, if they are strict observers of their faiths, will eat only meat from animals killed in this way. For Jews, the meat becomes kosher, and for Muslims, halal. Precise figures on the amount of such meat produced are difficult to find, but it is estimated that just over 91,000 cattle and more than 1½ million sheep and goats are killed this way in Britain each year.

Many people condemn this type of slaughter as barbaric, and would not dream of buying meat if they felt they might be supporting what appears to be appalling cruelty. But at least one in 10 ordinary leg of lamb joints, for instance, bought by non-Jews and non-Muslims, have been produced by religious slaughter methods. They are not labelled kosher or halal, and they are not on sale in obviously Jewish or Muslim food shops. Such meat may be in your local butcher's or your high street supermarket. There is no way to identify it, and no way to avoid it for those who wish to make a protest.

It is there mainly because the strictures of the Jewish method mean that all hindquarters and about a third of all forequarters are rejected because they are not good enough to be accepted as kosher. Jews are not allowed to eat hindquarter meat unless it has been 'porged' – a complicated process which involves removing some veins, lymph vessels and nerves – and since this has not been done since the 1930s all meat after the eleventh rib must be non-kosher. Forequarter meat may be rejected after the animal has been killed if any disease is found in the carcass. The slaughterhouse simply re-routes these rejected carcasses into the normal meat supply.

Diabolical! It's an understandable reaction from those who are neither Jewish nor Muslim, but just hang on before you reach any damning conclusions. The views on both sides of this heated argument are often ill-informed. Even some Jews and Muslims are confused about exactly what happens during the slaughter and on which religious principles it is based.

The traditions go way back into history, and it is probable that for both Jews and Muslims they were initially a way of making sure their meat was fit to eat. Both groups were also well in advance of their times in terms of compassion. In Old Testament times, animals would provide meat for the table in a most barbaric way . . . leg by leg. Because of the difficulties of storing meat, the cow or sheep would have a leg cut off, but to keep it alive, the blood vessels would be cauterized. It would be left to hobble until the next time meat was needed . . . and then it would lose another leg.

The Jewish code says that the animal must be healthy before slaughter and *must show no sign of injury*. This vital ruling is one of the stumbling blocks in the current debate, but ironically it almost certainly became part of the Jewish tradition in an attempt to outlaw that horrific cruelty. Other aspects of the Jewish rulings are also linked to the welfare of the animal. The slaughterman, known as the *shochet*, must be a Jew of good reputation and must use a long and extremely sharp knife. After each animal is killed, the knife must be sharpened again and inspected for any nick. This is to ensure that the cut is as painless as possible. If you can imagine the difference in pain after cutting yourself on a fine sharp razor, and cutting yourself on a serrated knife, you will understand the principle.

The precise methods which must be used to make sure meat is kosher have been handed down by word of mouth and written law from rabbi to rabbi. The ancient law which is often referred to is the Pentateuch (the first five books of the Old Testament), where, in *Deuteronomy* (12.21), it says, 'Thou shalt kill of thy herd and of thy flock, which the Lord hath given thee, as I have commanded thee . . .' It does not explain what that command was, but Jews believe it has been passed through the ages as a divine teaching. Then there's the Talmud, the code of Jewish religious, civil and social law, which gives instructions on how the carcass should be examined after death, to ensure that the animal was healthy. This involves making a cut in the side of the abdomen and feeling inside to check for any growths or other abnormalities.

The Muslim code is also based on concern for the animal. The same very sharp knife is used, and the animal should be in good health. The slaughterman, who must be a Muslim, recites the name of Allah at the moment of cutting the throat in order to remind himself of the weighty responsibility entrusted to him in taking the life of one of Allah's creatures. There is a lot of confusion about other aspects of the Muslim slaughter procedures. They vary from country to country, and even within Britain they vary from area to area. In general most Muslims believe the heart of the animal must be beating strongly when the throat is cut, in order to remove as much of the blood as possible. But this belief does not necessarily rule out stunning the animal into unconsciousness before the ritual, and in some Muslim slaughterhouses pre-stunning is part of the routine.

But it is the lack of any stunning in most Muslim and all Jewish slaughters which has concerned those who fight for the welfare of animals. The Jewish authorities insist that the animal cannot be stunned since it would then be injured before death and could not be classed as kosher. Many Muslims, too, believe their tradition would be invalid if the animal was unconscious before death, though others disagree. The Slaughterhouses Act 1974 says that animals which are to be bled to death must first be pre-stunned so that they are not conscious of any pain, but to accommodate religious beliefs, the Jewish and Muslim methods are exempted as long as the animal is being slaughtered to provide food for Jews or Muslims.

However, we have already seen that up to two-thirds of this meat goes on to the open market. Not only that, but more and more UK slaughterhouses are landing big export orders to supply halal meat to the Middle East. One of the biggest in recent years, from Libya, was reported to be worth £4 million, but of course the meat had to be produced according to Muslim tradition. The Meat and Livestock Commission is busily trying to net these valuable orders. At the huge Mefex '86 exhibition in Bahrain in February they had the biggest stand in the British pavilion, and reputedly were swamped with Arab buyers interested not just in our cuts of fresh beef and lamb, but also in meat products such as beefburgers. If the orders start to flow we can expect to see even more slaughterhouses being built to specialize in producing halal-killed meat.

In 1980 the growing number of British animals being slaughtered by religious methods prompted the Farm Animal Welfare Council to investigate the whole subject. And in a report published in July 1985, the Council called for changes within three years which would mean that all animals must be pre-stunned so that they could feel no pain, whatever the method of actual slaughter. It said: 'The up-to-date scientific evidence available and our own observations leave no doubt in our minds that religious methods of slaughter, even when carried out under ideal conditions, must result in a degree of pain, suffering and distress which does not occur in the properly stunned animal.'

At the start of 1986, the RSPCA also called for changes in methods which would require all slaughter without pre-stunning to be phased out. Religious slaughter, it said, 'causes pain and terror'. This would affect about ½ million Jews and about 1¼ million Muslims, the majority of whom are said to be strict observers of their faiths.

Members of the FAWC had visited a number of slaughter-houses to view the Jewish and Muslim methods and their report described in detail how the throat slitting was done. In the case of cattle, they said: 'The animal is restrained before slaughter in a casting pen so that it is on its back with its head resting on the ground and in a suitable position for the incision of its throat. The head must be held firmly to prevent the animal contributing to its own death. A single transverse cut must be made using a reciprocal motion of the knife . . . The intention is for the cut to produce an immediate outpouring of blood and this is achieved by severing both jugular veins and both carotid arteries . . . After the cut has been made the animal is pulled from the casting pen, shackled by a hind leg, and hoisted to continue the bleeding out process.'

Sheep are slaughtered in the same way, though they are not held tight in a casting pen but on a metal cradle, and the neck is extended in the right position by a helper. Poultry are held under the arm of the slaughterer while their throats are cut, and they are then left to bleed head downwards in a cone-shaped device. Pigs, of course, are never slaughtered in this way since neither Jews nor Muslims eat pork.

In response to the FAWC report, the Jewish and Muslim authorities have formed an unlikely alliance to try to convince the government of the humanity of their methods. They argue that the animal can feel no pain since the knife is so sharp it does not initially feel the cut; that by severing the two most important arteries and veins they cut off the blood supply to the head and that therefore the animal must immediately lose consciousness. Dr Majid Katme, president of the Islamic Medical Association and the author of the Muslim submission to the Ministry of Agriculture goes on to say, 'After a short resting phase, involuntary contractions and convulsions start and occur as automatic physiological reflexes in order to push blood up to the deprived brain. These reactions and convulsions are painless.' Both groups cite scientific research which shows that the animal suffers no more by their methods than it would if it were first stunned.

But the Welfare Council disagrees. For a start, it claims that the cutting technique of the slaughterman is not always perfect. 'It was evident that there was a great variation in the degree of expertise used when making the throat incision . . . Particular examples, seen in Muslim slaughter, included one occasion when a deep cut was made which almost severed the head of an animal; in another case the spinal column was severed. Sometimes the knife was not sufficiently sharp and there was difficulty making the cut.

'We observed that the "single transverse cut" demanded by the Jews means in practice a backwards and forwards stroke. On one occasion we observed a Jewish slaughterman making as many as seven backwards and forwards strokes with the knife, using a sawing action.'

The Council also argues that while it is virtually impossible to prove, by scientific means, at what point the animal can no longer feel pain, all the signs are that loss of consciousness starts nine to 11 seconds after the cut. However, as losing

51

consciousness and feeling pain are gradual processes, it is possible that a sheep may be sensitive to pain on average 14 seconds after the cut, and calves 17 seconds after the cut.

But the Council points out that these measurements were taken in scientific conditions, whereas 'Our observations during visits to slaughterhouses have shown that following less expert slaughter, where the cuts have been less effectively carried out, animals have apparently remained conscious for much longer periods than these.'

What worries the animal welfare people is not only that the animal must feel pain from the cut on its neck, but also that some may be hoisted on to the conveyor to hang upside down while still aware of their plight. 'In some cases, both with Jewish and Muslim slaughter, we considered that animals were pulled out of the pen too quickly and before they were fully unconscious,' says the report. 'In one particular case, cattle were shackled and hoisted very quickly after throat-cutting and the incision made by the Jewish inspector to examine the thoracic cavity was made less than one minute after the animal's throat was cut. On another occasion we saw the animal recoil when the *shochet* attempted to shackle it. Sheep were always shackled and hoisted immediately. In many cases we have not been satisfied that the thoracic examination carried out in Jewish religious slaughter commenced *after* the animal was dead and therefore the stated practice [*the Jewish code decrees that the animal must be dead before examination*] was not found to be the norm.

'We are concerned that some animals may be subjected to shackling, hoisting, thoracic incision and internal examination while they still retain some degree of sensitivity.'

The last main worry was the way in which cattle approached their death. In normal slaughter techniques the animal is driven into a stunning box where it cannot move, but where it remains on its feet until knocked unconscious. With religious methods, the animals are pinioned into a casting pen. These are huge metal crates with moving sides which crush to the animal's size. Once pinned in the right position with its head protruding from the front, the whole crate is revolved through half a circle, so that the animal is lying on its back with its head upturned on the floor.

In this position the throat can be more easily cut and the blood will flow away faster. But the Council team found this procedure terrified most of the cattle who were its victims. Cows and calves are afraid of confined spaces and the time spent locked in the crate before the slaughterman did his job was long enough to cause extreme distress to the occupant. The strange sensation of revolving also caused panic, and worse than that, because lying upside down is totally unnatural to cattle it may cause pain.

'Any ruminant placed on its back suffers gross discomfort due to the weight and size of the rumen with its contents pressing upon the diaphragm and thoracic organs,' says the report. 'With one exception, the manner of operation of the pens we saw was unsatisfactory, particularly the momentum once the rotation had begun, and the lack of an adequate braking system, which resulted in the pen swinging initially through more than 180 degrees and rocking backwards and forwards before stabilizing. Apart from the question of actual infliction of pain we are acutely aware of the terror and discomfort which ensue from the inversion of cattle followed by forcible extension of the neck, often resulting in the animal banging its head on the floor. When the pen is in position, the animal's head is usually restrained by the foot of an operator or by a rope halter; on one occasion, because of the violent movement of the animal's head two or three operators were required to hold the head steady before the slaughterman made the incision. On some occasions we witnessed animals being held in this position for longer than we found acceptable because the slaughterman was not always ready to do the cutting.'

The FAWC told the government it should ban these pens and insist that an American upright version be used for religious slaughter instead. Called an ASPCA-type (because it was approved by the US equivalent of the RSPCA) it has a more open design, but still supports the animal firmly, holding it under the belly and chin. In this way the animal does not have to be revolved at all, which must go at least some way to relieving its distress.

One other form of religious slaughter is allowed in Britain, though it is not much used. Many Sikhs will only eat meat if it has been killed by decapitation. This is allowed under the present law since the Slaughterhouses Act 1974 states that animals must either be stunned before slaughter or 'slaughtered instantaneously by means of a mechanically operated instrument in proper repair'. In practice some animals, mainly sheep and poultry, are killed by use of a guillotine, and they can then be declared 'jhatka'. In fact many Sikhs are vegetarian, and very few eat beef, so it is thought that very little meat is produced this way. Nevertheless research has shown that decapitation does not mean instant oblivion for the animal. According to the FAWC, the method should be banned and the law changed to insist that all food animals are stunned before they are killed.

While stunning sounds humane, the problem for the animal welfare campaigners has been its unreliability. Time and again religious groups have defended their methods by attacking the alternative. Quite rightly, they have pointed out that if stunning is not done efficiently it can be little better than torture.

The captive bolt pistol (so called because the bullet can be retrieved each time) has always been thought of as a thoroughly dependable method. The idea is that the bolt causes instant brain death, and although the heart may carry on beating for some time, the animal is oblivious to any pain. But the method relies on the operator hitting the animal squarely between the eyes, and this is not always easy. Although a stunning pen is used, many heifers, bullocks and calves are so upset at being parted from their mates that they jump around and toss their heads in fright. If they cannot make a clear shot from the front, some handlers approach from behind and use the pistol to shoot forwards from behind the ears. The animal will keel over in just the same way, but it may be that the bullet has caused total paralysis and only temporary stunning. One RSPCA inspector recalled a terrifying occasion when the beast was so badly shot that it got up and chased the handlers round the slaughterhouse.

It must be said that these incidents are few and far between. According to the veterinary profession, which has to oversee them, most slaughterhouses are conscientious and the captive bolt is the most effective stunning method we have. But one creature who regains consciousness and feels pain is one too many, and any improvements that can be made to make this system 100 per cent reliable would be welcomed by the millions of meat-eaters, and ought to be pressed for by the government on our behalf. However, no matter how reliable the process, it is highly unlikely that religious groups would accept it as part of their ritual since their laws demand that the animal is uninjured when it approaches its death.

A far more practical possibility is stunning by mild electrocution, which is used mainly for calves, pigs and sheep at the moment. Since the unconsciousness is only temporary this has been proposed as a method which, it might be argued, would not go against the religious law which demands that the animal be in good health and free from injury. The electric current usually does the animal no long-term harm, and in theory it could be running around in perfect health a few minutes later if it were to be granted a reprieve. But this short-term effect is itself problematic.

The animal is given the shock through the temples with a pair of electrified tongs which make contact on each side of the head. But some woolly-faced sheep often do not receive a strong enough current because the wool acts as an insulator. Sometimes the operators get sloppy and do not position the electrodes in the right place. Sometimes they are just in a rush and do not hold them in place long enough. Whatever the cause, it is known that some animals may recover consciousness too soon, as they are trundled along the conveyor towards the sticking area.

Electrical stunning often does not last long enough anyway. On average, the animal will be unconscious for 20 seconds, but a Food Research Institute study of the length of time between stunning and sticking showed it was often 30 seconds, and could be as long as a minute if something went wrong on the line.

Poultry may die a horrible death, too. They are always stunned, not with tongs, but by being drawn through a water bath which is electrified. Then their necks are cut either manually or by machine, and they go into a scalding tank to loosen their feathers. But lots of things can go wrong. First, hung by the legs, some birds are shorter than others and their heads may miss the live water altogether. In some cases the slaughterhouse does not use a strong enough current in the water bath and so birds may recover quickly afterwards. Sometimes the neck-cutting machinery does not work properly, and misses a few birds, or does not cut deeply enough. All in all, there is no doubt a few of those cling-wrapped offerings in the supermarket have met a pitiful end.

It goes to show that despite our faith in modern machinery, humane methods and the power of the law, some animals still go through unbelievable suffering to satisfy our demand for meat. It is important that people who eat meat realize that slaughtering methods are far from perfect so that public opinion can be harnessed to goad the meat industry into reaching for the highest standards. The only encouraging thought is that at least our systems are improving. Each time a new slaughterhouse is built, or an old plant invests in some new machinery, the lot of our food animals improves. But it will not all happen voluntarily. Without a government which is brave enough to intervene, animals will still be cruelly turned on their backs and have their throats cut while they are wide awake. And unless the Minister of Agriculture has the moral courage to insist, at the very least, that meat produced in this way is properly labelled 'killed while conscious', 'unstunned', or 'slaughtered by religious methods', there will be nothing consumers can do to protest.

4

The tender trap

Anyone with an ounce of consideration for animals would wish their last moments to be as pleasant as possible. If they have to die, then there should be no pain and no mental anguish attached to that death. Most of us would be outraged to know that a process exists which distresses the animal just before it is stunned, and which is done for no better reason than to make its meat more tender for us to eat.

Some slaughterhouses now inject live animals with a special tenderizing solution a few minutes before they are stunned and killed. They have to be trapped and held still in a special 'cattle crush' or box while the solution goes into the bloodstream, through a type of drip mechanism. The substance is in fact an enzyme produced from the juices of the papaya tree, and only one company, Beatrice Swifts (of Butterball fame), holds the patent.

One vet who works at a slaughterhouse where cattle are tenderized reported to the British Veterinary Association that the injection could bring on a state of toxic shock. In January 1985 the Animal Welfare Committee of the BVA heard that 'at least once a day' animals appeared to collapse with some sort of anaphylactic shock.

Other firms use similar enzyme solutions, but never on live animals. They may be used to tenderize cuts of meat – by injecting a steak or joint, say, with the solution through a bank of fine needles. Some sell it in the form of a tenderizing marinade for the consumer to use in the kitchen, and others offer it in the form of a powder to shake over meat before cooking. But none of these methods is particularly successful since the meat tends to react to the enzyme in patches, and may come out tough in some places and mushy in others.

Pawpaw has long been known to be a good meat tenderizer. Five hundred years ago the Mexican Indians hit on the idea of wrapping their meat in the leaves of the papaya tree to make it less tough. Pineapple and figs contain the same enzyme (that is the reason why the practice of serving gammon and pineapple became popular). Now Swifts have brought the technique up to date and sell the right to make use of their patent to slaughterhouses who can then market the extra-tender meat under the 'Proten' label, if they wish.

The papaya enzyme they use, called papain, works by speeding up the maturing process. Normally, meat needs to be hung so that natural enzymes, called proteolytic enzymes, within it help to break down the muscle structure and 'mature' it. This is why traditional butchers always talk fondly of well-hung beef – they know that after two or three weeks' hanging time it will be deliciously tender. The enzymes from the pawpaw work in the same way, but their great advantage is that there is no waiting time. Slaughterhouses and butchers do not have to leave their capital tied up for weeks while nature takes its course. The enzyme will do its job in the hour or so when the meat starts to cook since it is activated when the temperature reaches about 150 degrees centigrade. In theory, meat which is tenderized and slaughtered one day may be eaten the next.

Surprisingly, for a natural product, a huge amount of secrecy surrounds this technique. The Federation of Fresh Meat Wholesalers, who represent slaughterhouses, admitted they were 'cagey about discussing such things' and could not give any information. The patent-holders, Swifts, who not only make poultry products but also run a chain of slaughterhouses, refused to discuss the process with the author on the telephone, demanded questions in writing, and insisted on a face-to-face interview before they would come up with any answers. They also refused a request by the author to witness the procedure.

They insisted that their technique had no effect on the animal before slaughter at all. But they refused to explain any of the details concerning how the enzyme was administered or how much was given. They would not reveal how many slaughterhouses used it, nor how much of our meat had been treated. They had to protect the secrets of the patent from rivals, they said. With the process being publicly available for all to see at the Patents Office in London, it was a puzzling explanation.

If you read patent numbers 913202 and 913203 you start to understand why Swifts might prefer to keep the details of their technique under wraps. They explain that in the past tenderizing methods used on carcass meat were not very successful because the enzyme was not distributed very well: 'The resulting product has over-tenderized or mushy spots with other portions of the meat having little or no tenderization due to insufficient distribution of the enzyme solution in the capillary beds of the muscle tissue.'

But Swifts have the answer. 'The present invention relates to the ante-mortem injection of a proteolytic enzyme into the vascular system of an animal, and the holding of the animal for a period of time to attain distribution of the enzyme throughout the vascular system before slaughter.' The enzyme solution is injected into the jugular vein in the neck with 'a needle, tube and gravity-flow bottle' according to the patent.

The lengthy document goes on to explain that live chickens, lambs, beef animals, pigs and calves can be tenderized, though of course the amount of enzyme varies according to the size of the animal and the chosen strength of the solution. If the enzyme powder makes up only one per cent of the solution, then it will take a lot of liquid to tenderize a large animal such as a cow. 'In some cases volumes of approximately 2.5 litres of the enzyme solution must be injected into the animal,' says the patent. 'A five per cent solution of the enzyme, on the other hand, may be much more conveniently used since only about 500 ml of this solution are required to inject an average animal with a desirable amount.' It would seem then, from the patent, that the 'average' animal (the term is not defined) has to absorb just under a pint of solution to be satisfactorily tenderized. But some grades of stock, it says, need a lot more enzyme than this. Old ewes which have come to the end of their lambing days, and dairy cows which have been drained of their last drop of milk, will inevitably be tougher and need more tenderizing.

Swifts say their process is used only for prime beef cattle in Britain, and although they would not reveal how large the injection needed to be, vets who have seen the treatment report that it consists of about 200 ml of diluted enzyme which takes considerably longer than an average injection to administer.

The reason this objectionable process works so well is that the animal's own blood system spreads the solution evenly throughout its own flesh. There are no pockets of mushiness since the heavy concentration of enzyme in the main veins and arteries is drained away when the animal is bled. 'The maze of smaller vessels consisting of the arterioles, capillaries, and venules is drained only slightly, if at all, in the bleeding step and hence holds the blood containing the distributed enzyme in the meat. Thus, the meat has a substantially uniform distribution of enzymes therein,' says the patent.

This can only be achieved if the creature is forced to wait a few minutes after the injection so that its body can work the magic scientists cannot achieve by other means. Only then may it be slaughtered. According to the patent, the delay may be from one to 30 minutes, although a four-hour wait is possible. In their ideal method 'the animal is then held for six to fifteen minutes before slaughter to give adequate distribution of the enzyme to all portions of the carcass and provide desirable control of the enzyme tenderizing action,' i.e. uniformity of tenderization between roasts and steaks or chops.

Perhaps Swifts' reluctance to discuss the way they tenderize meat stems from a damning report of the process by the Farm Animal Welfare Council in 1984. Representatives from the Council watched animals being given the enzyme at two slaughterhouses, and in the first-hand account that follows it presents a graphic description of how the patent works in practice.

'Immediately prior to slaughter the animal is driven into a crush and the head tied and pulled up in such a way that the neck is extended for presentation of the vein for the injection. Assessment of the dosage (which is based on weight of the animal) and the injection process is carried out by lay slaughterhouse staff who are given specific training in the technique. In one slaughterhouse, one of two animals seen resisted restraint of its head so violently that attempts to inject it had to be abandoned.

'Our concern is with the principle of the whole process rather than with its method of application i.e. whether it is an unnecessary interference to the animal which affects its welfare at the time of slaughter. There is also a possibility that tissue degeneration, although not common, can occur.

'We consider there is a real risk that animals can suffer as a result of the process, particularly if subsequent slaughter has to be delayed. We therefore recommend that the technique should be banned.'

Yet Swifts insist that the animal feels nothing at the time of the injection, and is not affected by the enzyme in any way. Although Swifts use the process only on beef animals, an old but interesting piece of research by the Americans McCluskey and Thomas in 1958 showed that the enzyme did have an unusual effect on rabbits: when the tenderizer was given to them while alive their ears drooped.

More recent research, Swifts claim, has given the process a clean bill of health. They point to the Ministry of Agriculture's answer to the FAWC report, which, they say, clears them of any charge of cruelty. In fact, the Ministry's official answer refers to work done by its own laboratory which shows that the enzyme has no effect on the animal immediately after injection. The document states: 'There is no evidence that tissue deterioration occurs in animals slaughtered within a few minutes.' But no amount of research can show what the animal feels. And if the injection really has no effect on it, why is it that a vet reports that some animals appear to collapse with toxic shock? In any case, whether the animal does, or does not, feel anything from queasiness to pain after the

61

injection is not the central point. Both Swifts and the Ministry have ignored the main basis of the Council's objection – that the whole procedure is unnecessary and distressing for the animal.

As far as our own welfare goes, there is no evidence that the residue of papain in the meat will do us any harm. It is, after all, what we would consume if we ate a pawpaw.

Strangely, however, few butchers appear to like the process and the 'Proten' brand name is rarely seen, despite the fact that Swifts say the technique is now widespread. The explanation may be that some butchers buy tenderized beef but prefer not to shout about it. Perhaps it is enough for them that the consumer finds their meat always tender and so becomes a loyal customer.

The meat trade's secrecy on the subject has been so effective that few consumers are aware that such a controversial method exists, much less that they might well have been eating the results of the process. By law, the only indication that meat has been subjected to this treatment is the word 'tenderized'. But since this is sometimes used on the label of steaks that have been bashed with a mallet, and joints made from meat which has been flaked and re-formed (see Chapter 8), as well as meat which has been tenderized *after* death, the consumer has no way of distinguishing pre-slaughter tenderized meat.

This silly confusion is the result of the recent Food Labelling Regulations which decided that the word 'tenderized' was a suitable way to describe any meat that had been injected with enzymes. Swifts say, revealingly perhaps, that they are quite happy with the description and would not want to make the labelling any more precise. But their governing body, the Meat and Livestock Commission, disagrees.

'We objected very strongly to this part of the Labelling Regulations because we felt that a general word was being used to describe widely different processes,' said its spokesman Geoff Harrington. 'A lot of retailers don't like the idea of this enzyme-treated meat and we feel the customer should be able to make an informed choice.'

The FAWC has told the Minister that this unnecessary treatment should be banned, but so far he has ignored the Council's view. In his official answer to its report he says, 'There is insufficient justification for such a ban.'

While most of us are kept in the dark about it he can afford to sweep the issue under the carpet. But it is time we heard the truth about the price of tenderness. If Swifts can defend their method, let them remove the wraps and talk openly about what is involved. And at the very least, consumers should be told when they are buying 'live tenderized' meat, whether it is from the supermarket, the butcher's, or the works canteen. That way, anyone who objects can take their custom elsewhere. Then Swifts might be forced to think again . . . and try a little tenderness.

5

Dyes and disguise

The tenderizing injection is just one of many extras added to meat at various stages in the meat machine's progress. By the time it reaches the slaughterhouse, it may contain drug residues, a legacy of modern farming methods, too. But these pale into virtual insignificance against the huge amount of additives which will go in during the manufacturing process.

The threat posed by chemical additives in our food is one of the biggest concerns of the 'eighties. We now recognize the possibility of long-term danger to our health by eating some chemicals, and the short-term problems of toxic and allergic effects from others. An astonishing array of additives goes into our food. Some are necessary. But a huge number with no useful function to perform have been implicated in allergic reactions. Colourings are probably the most obvious unnecessary additive, and yet they are found in almost all types of food in vast quantities. Doctors are certain that some of them cause hyperactivity in children, and may be the trigger for asthma, hayfever and skin rashes.

Many mothers are now very aware of the problems, and keep a wary eye on the ingredients list as they do their weekly shopping. Criticism has centred on products such as snack foods, instant desserts, sweets and soft drinks. Few people would immediately think of meat as a culprit. It comes as some surprise to discover that meat products are number two in the league table of coloured foods. We eat more coloured meat than we do coloured sweets or snacks. The only food category representing a higher concentration of colourings is soft drinks.

Apart from drug residues and natural enzymes fresh meat

must not by law, contain any additives at all. But there is no such restriction on the makers of burgers, sausages or pâté, even though they may be displayed alongside joints, steaks and chops in the supermarket cabinet. Many of the manufactured meats are in fact heavily laced with colour, flavour and preservative.

The regular – and shocking – revelations of recent years about what goes into our food have served to make many of us think that additives are something new . . . the products of our hi-tech way of living. Yet even Iron Age man used science to create new food products, and the subject of his experiments was meat. A thousand years before Christ, man discovered that he could preserve his meat through the long winter by covering it in salt. He did not understand the chemistry behind his invention, but he did know that this additive meant his family were less likely to go hungry or to die because they did not have enough to eat. Meat, in fact, was probably one of the first foods to receive added chemicals.

Since then we have developed over 3,500 different chemicals for preserving, colouring, thickening, sweetening, stabilizing, emulsifying and flavouring. Until now, foods like the instant desserts and snack foods have claimed most of our attention, simply because of the very long lists of additives with which they are associated. One well-known instant trifle has no less than 31 different additives! By comparison only a limited number of added chemicals goes into meat products, but those that do should give us just as much to worry about. Not only do we eat them in large quantities, but processed meat attracts a selection of some of the most controversial additives permitted by the government.

By far the most popular colour used in meat products is Red 2G. But it has been tentatively linked with cancer, and can be the cause of allergies and sensitive reactions in people who eat it or work with it. The foods industries in the USA and the rest of the EEC do not use it. Yet the British government continues to allow manufacturers to put any amount of it into our food. Bacon, ham and gammon contain nitrites, used in curing to preserve meat from harmful bacteria. But they have been shown to cause cancer in animals and have been cited as a possible cause of cancer and diabetes in man.

Finally, there is monosodium glutamate, known by its more sinister-sounding shortform, MSG. Because of its atrocious record of causing intolerant reactions in some people, it is not approved by the EEC. Countless numbers of people have suffered the severe headaches, nausea, dizziness and palpitations which this flavour enhancer is known to cause. Yet the British government sets no limits on its use.

These three dubious chemicals are not the only ones used in meat products and not all meat products contain them. But they are by far the most common, and are used in huge quantities. What makes meat products different from so many other foods is that they are more likely to include one or more

Coloured foods that form part of the average diet

	Intake per day in grammes
Soft drinks	216
Meat products	44
Flour confectionery	41
Butter and margarine	37
Canned vegetables	32
Chocolates and sweets	16
Cheese	15
Canned fruit	15
Breakfast cereals	12
Canned soup	12
Preserves	8
Dessert mixes	8
Snack foods	7

Source: Food Additives and Contaminants Committee Report, 1979

of this trio of the most questionable additives than they are any others. And apart from the potential health risks posed by each of them, what has never been investigated is the possibility of a 'molotov cocktail' effect caused by mixing them all together.

Among the other little extras in meat products are colours, like the notorious tartrazine, as well as caramel, sunset yellow, carmoisine, erythrosine, cochineal; various polyphosphates; anti-oxidants, such as sodium ascorbate, vitamin C, vitamin E; preservatives, such as sulphur dioxide, sodium sulphite and sodium metabisulphite; and stabilizers, such as guar gum.

All of them must now be shown on the ingredients list, either by number or by name. The EEC has provided a comprehensive system for identifying all the main categories of additives, apart from flavourings. Those additives which have passed safety tests are recommended for use by the EEC's Scientific Committee and appear on its 'approved' list, though member countries have a great deal of leeway when it comes to following that guidance. Britain has been particularly noisy in lobbying for more additives to be included so that its own manufacturers would not be forced to abandon their traditional ingredients.

The real scandal that the food industry has done its best to deny is that so many of these additives are quite unnecessary. In many cases, but especially in meat products, they are used to deceive the customer as to the true quality of what she is buying. Because the industry does not fill its steak-and-kidney pies with much real steak, or its pork sausages with much lean pork, or its beefburgers with a high proportion of top-quality beef (at least, not often!) it needs to rely on extra colouring and flavouring to kid us that it has.

If added colour was not allowed the customer would be able to spot on sight the beef sausage manufacturer who pads out his products with scraps from turkey carcasses, or worse, with extra fat. Against a top-quality sausage made with generous quantities of lean beef his would look pale and wan. What a tragedy for profits! So he uses an artificial red colouring to give the impression that his sausage is as meaty as the next man's.

We have come to accept added colourings as natural ingredients in food. However, next time you give a new pair of jeans their final rinse, ask yourself how much you'd fancy drinking that dark blue water. The fact is that most of us could easily take in that much dye in our everyday foodstuffs. Because, to all intents and purposes, our food is *dyed*, and many of the chemicals used are no different from those that colour our clothes, curtains and carpets.

Flavourings, too, are particularly important to meat-product makers. Although we cannot see the difference on the supermarket shelf, any manufacturer who puts lots of ground-up gristle, fat or sinew in his pork pies, for instance, would be found out on taste. To protect himself he adds MSG to bring out the flavour of the little bit of lean pork that is in the pie. The problem is that these corner-cutting firms may use so many chemicals to such good effect that the next man's truly meaty pork pie starts to look like the poor relation. And that is why even the manufacturers of good-quality meat products have had to bend to the current fashion of putting the contents of a chemistry set into our food.

The food industry has always defended its behaviour by pointing out the safety function of additives. Without them food would go bad, and might poison us, they say. This is quite true. Some preservatives are vital, but they are only a tiny proportion of all the additives used, and certainly do not merit the degree of emphasis they have been given in the debate. Manufacturers spend 40 times more money on flavourings than they do on preservatives, for example, and eight times more on colourings. Even flavour enhancers are five times more important in money terms than preservatives. Yet whenever the industry counters its critics it trots out the preservatives argument in prime position. It knows it's on to a winner.

When up against the anti-additive campaigners, the Food and Drink Federation, which represents food manufacturers, has constantly pressed the need for additives on the grounds of safety. One press statement issued in December 1985 typifies its stance: 'Manufacturers' primary concern is for the safety of food products. Not only are permitted food additives subject to repeated vigorous testing but certain of them are also important for keeping products themselves safe and in good condition.'

And in a glossy brochure meant to smooth over the public's fears, the Chemical Industries Association (which represents the firms who make the additives) reminds us of the risks of doing without some of their substances.

It states (note the order): 'The major categories of additives are: preservatives, antioxidants, emulsifiers, stabilizers, colours, and flavouring agents.'

And it goes on to say: 'Preservatives are perhaps the most important food additives. Food can be colonized by bacteria and fungi which produce deadly poisons: Salmonella and Clostridium (botulinium) are the most notorious of the bacteria and many moulds produce aflatoxins, which are powerful cancer-inducers.'

The Food and Drink Industries Council again puts preservatives top of its list of 'major uses' in a booklet on food additives issued in 1983. But this claim can only apply to a small proportion of the substances added to our food.

According to additives campaigner Melanie Miller, of the London Food Commission, only 1,600 tonnes of preservatives go into our food each year, together with about 100 tonnes of anti-oxidants, which prevent fats going rancid. In contrast, between 35,000 and 45,000 tonnes of flavourings are used, 6,500 tonnes of flavour-enhancers and 9000 tonnes of colours. It is estimated that each man, woman and child eats between 8 and 11 lbs of additives a year, on average, which is the equivalent of 12 grammes a day. About a quarter will be flavourings, flavour-enhancers and colourings, and a fifth will be thickeners and stabilizers. Only a sixth will be nutrients and vitamins, and less than one-hundredth will be preservatives and anti-oxidants.

Estimate of food additive use, 1984

Categories	Quantity (tonnes per year)
Flavours	35–45,000
Thickeners and stabilizers	41,000
Nutrients and vitamins	30,000+
Emulsifiers and surfactants	27,000
Acids	25,000
Colours	9,000
Enzymes	8,000
Flavour-enhancers	6,500
Sweeteners	2,500+
Preservatives	1,600+
Anti-oxidants	100+
Other	10,000+

NB: flavours include the weight of liquid 'carriers'
Source: London Food Commission

Another favourite argument used frequently by the food and additive industries is that everything we eat is made up of chemicals, and there are far more undesirable substances in natural foods than in what is added to them. The CIA booklet says: 'Chemical names may sound forbidding, but they are just a way of naming and classifying the huge numbers of known chemical substances . . . Natural foodstuffs differ from laboratory chemicals mainly in the bewildering mixtures of substances that they contain – 42 chemical substances have been identified in orange oil extracted from orange peel . . . Recently, many food additives have been suspected of causing allergies or intolerances in small susceptible groups of people. It is worth remembering that the millions of such sufferers today are mostly susceptible to natural products: hay-fever sufferers are affected by the proteins in pollen grains; coeliacs by the gluten in wheat; others react to strawberries or shellfish.'

The theory seems to be that since natural things cause allergies, there is no reason why the food industry should not add a few unnatural items to the list of potential allergens. The difference is that by doing so they stop a sensitive person from eating everything to which that allergen has been added, not just from one obvious group of foods such as shellfish, or milk products, which is known to them. Many people have to spend a great deal of time in the supermarket reading the ingredients lists if they want to keep themselves, or a member of their family, healthy. What makes most consumers angry is that more and more people are suffering some sort of allergy not because they are unluckily sensitive to a natural food, but because they are sensitive to something which exists in what they eat only in order to boost a company's profits.

Where a chemical has a vital safety function and cannot be replaced by a safer alternative, few campaigners would argue that it should be banned unless the evidence against it were overwhelming. Then, perhaps, the products containing it should be withdrawn. And few people would demand a ban on chemicals that genuinely did add to the quality of our food if thorough safety tests showed no sign of a health risk.

What the experts do question is the continued use of chemicals about which there are reasonable health doubts, which have no value for the customer, and which may actually mislead us as to the true nature of the food. There are far more such chemicals than there are additives with a vital role to play and the food industry's various clever arguments have never succeeded in defending their use. Nowhere are they more obvious than in the meat products business.

Red 2G

For some experts, it is a source of constant astonishment that this dye is still being used in large quantities in our food. Its purpose is frequently to mislead the consumer by making meat products appear meatier than they really are. Doctors believe it makes sensitive children hyper-active, causes skin rashes and purple patches, and gives some people hay fever-like symptoms. And that's just for starters. One or two studies have shown that Red 2G might be a possible cause of cancer in animal tests, and may cause genetic changes in the body's cells. Like many of the tests on additives, they have so far proved inconclusive, and on the balance of evidence consumers must presume it is safe.

In the United States it is not included in food at all, and the Scientific Committee of the EEC has steadfastly refused to approve its use. That is why the dye is not entitled to have an E placed before its official number, 128. (In fact, a few supermarkets, presumably through ignorance, do label it as E128, but this is quite wrong). France, West Germany and most of the other member countries have agreed with the committee's conclusions and have banned Red 2G from their food products. But the British food industry has gained a special exemption which gives it the right to continue using this questionable chemical in our food.

Not only that, but the Ministry of Agriculture has been lobbying for the EEC to change its mind and put Red 2G on its permitted list. At present, it has been added to a shortlist of colours which are under scrutiny for approval. However, further tests have not cleared the doubts surrounding Red 2G and some have only served to confirm in the minds of a few experts the fears that it may be a possible link with cancer. With controversy still raging about its safety, it seems unlikely that the EEC will be persuaded to go back on its earlier conviction.

Red 2G is an artificial chemical dye produced from coal tar. It is used not only in food, but also in the woollen industry. Sausages and sweaters may have one thing in common – they may both be dyed pink using Red 2G. Many coal tar dyes, known as azo dyes, are a common cause of allergic and sensitive reactions, especially in children. One Welsh mother's experience is typical of many.

Sam had a healthy appetite just like most other 6-year-olds, apart from one thing . . . he could not eat sausages. Just one was enough to bring on a seizure. Yet he could eat fresh meats, mince and pies without any problem. His mother, Louise, soon learned to cut sausages out of his diet and put Sam's problem down to one of the additives they contained. It could not have been the preservatives or the polyphosphates, since Sam could eat ham, cold meat and all other meat products quite happily. Louise decided it could only be the colouring, but it was not until Sam's sixth birthday that she proved her hunch was almost certainly right. More than anything else he wanted sausages for his birthday tea, and as a special treat Louise bought some additive-free sausages. Then she just crossed her fingers. Sam was fine, though an experiment a few days later showed he was still allergic to the traditional pink sausage.

It is not only children who may be allergic to the extras in manufactured meat. One woman nearly died after eating a slice of delicatessen sausage, because she was sensitive to one of the additives. As the owner of a butcher's shop herself, she is now not only careful what she eats, but also what she sells to other people.

When the sausage was delivered that morning the meat company's rep had told Pat it was a 'new, improved' version. The preservatives and flavour were the same but the colour was much brighter. So after slicing off half a pound for a customer, Pat tasted it. There was just half a slice left over on the cutter, but it was enough to put Pat flat on her back for four days. 'Half an hour after this little taste I felt giddy, violently sick and very weak. Then I passed out. The doctor said that I was allergic to the colouring and it was a good job I had not eaten a proper slice. Now I'm very careful not to eat food with chemical colourings, especially meat products, and I won't sell anything that I know is highly coloured to my customers.'

Red 2G is the most commonly found dye in meat products. Everything from sausages to veal escalopes, fresh beefburgers to faggots are likely to bear its rosy hue. Manufacturers say they cannot use anything else. Because fresh meat products are wrapped in see-through film the colourings used must be stable in light. Products laced with Red 2G stay as pink as the day they were packed, whereas other colours would fade and go patchy, they claim.

In fact, Red 2G is one of the cheaper artificial dyes, and this may explain why some manufacturers cannot bear to be parted from it. Other firms have proved that it is not irreplaceable. For example, Marks & Spencer uses the natural but expensive red colouring cochineal in its sausages. 'We are aware that the rest of the high street tends to use Red 2G in sausages, but we prefer cochineal because it is natural,' said a spokeswoman. 'It does fade more quickly when exposed to light but this is not a problem for us since our sausages have a short shelf-life of just six days from the day of manufacture to the last day of sale.' Other firms like their sausages to last from ten days to three weeks before they have to be sold.

But why do sausages have to be dyed in the first place? If you take an objective look at most brands on the shop shelves they are a distinctly unnatural shade of pink. After all, pork *should* be more beige than pink, and it certainly should not look puce. But uncoloured sausages can be found. Some butchers are experimenting with additive-free versions, one or two supermarkets have dropped colour from their own-label sausages, and there are even a few special-recipe versions from branded manufacturers in the supermarkets which do not need colour. Look, for example, at Lincolnshire sausages: these are generally made with no dye and are therefore paler when compared with the traditional pork or beef varieties, but the flecks of green herbs create the visual interest manufacturers believe we expect.

Any manufacturer who makes a genuinely meaty sausage should not need to dye it pink. According to one butcher who makes additive-free sausages, 'the meat will show through. Beef sausages are a totally different colour to pork. They come out quite a dark, dusky shade of pink – almost red – while pork sausages are a pinky fawn colour. I can't understand how consumers are taken in by these pasty pink things that call themselves sausages. We use a 95-per-cent meat mixture in our sausages, of which about 10 per cent will be fat. You can see the chunks of meat inside and they give the colour. But these big manufacturers often cream the meat in high-pressure machines, using a large proportion of fat, rind and various bits of colourless offals, and of course, their final product looks a horrible shade of grey. Beef and pork sausages come out much the same so they try to put back the difference by using a bit more red dye in the beef. It doesn't fool me and I wish it didn't fool the people who buy them but until they've seen a really meaty sausage they'll never know the difference.'

More butchers and small manufacturers might try dye-free sausages if it were not for the ready-mixed seasonings which so often contain colouring. They are almost always bought in by the small-scale maker, who has neither the time nor the expertise to mix his own. These give him little option but to turn out pink products. Although one seasoning manufacturer is rumoured to be planning to drop dyes from his mixture, at the moment 'white seasoning', as it is called, is hard to find.

Unlike some other additives, there is no restriction on the types of products which may be given the Red 2G treatment and no upper limit on the amount which may be used. This means some people, particularly children, the elderly and those on low incomes, may take in above average amounts of the dye if they eat cheaper processed forms of meat rather than fresh meat.

It would be very useful to know which brands use a lot of Red 2G, and which use only a pinch. The Ministry of Agriculture knows, but may not reveal the information: it is an Official Secret. A few years ago a ministry committee, the Food Advisory Committee, called for a brand-by-brand listing of the amounts of colouring used in each item of food. The manufacturers' association gathered these embarrassing facts from its members and the fascinating results are now being considered by the committee.

According to one committee member, the differences between products are 'quite staggering'. One manufacturer uses ten times more dye in the same type of meat product than a rival. If we only knew who that was, sensitive people and those worried about the possible cancer hazard could at least avoid eating large quantities of Red 2G.

It is not easy to spot the highly dyed products on the

supermarket shelves. While two packs of sausages, say, may look an unnaturally strong shade of pink, one may have a generous amount of lean beef with just a touch of colouring, and the other may be saturated with dye to cover up for its lack of lean meat. Only a sausage with no colouring at all and plenty of lean meat will be easy to recognize by its colour.

The ingredients list is not much help either. Although the contents must be listed in descending order of weight, because colourings are added as powders they will almost invariably appear bottom of the list. Even when they are used in huge quantities, they are still likely to be lighter in weight than other additives such as preservatives or emulsifiers.

It is a tragedy for consumers that they will never be allowed to know which manufacturer loads his meat products with red dye and which uses merely a trace. For while the committee members themselves are not strictly covered by the Official Secrets Act, the documents they have been working with are. They are currently reviewing the use of all colourings and are due to report at the end of 1986. But even then it is unlikely that the levels of dye in particular brands of food will be revealed. Despite a slight relaxation of the secrecy rules in the summer of 1986, the dye ist remains sacrosanct: manufacturers have already been guaranteed confidentiality. The most the consumer will be permitted to know will probably be the range of amounts used in general classes of products. So the makers of highly dyed foods can sleep easy in their beds.

Monosodium glutamate

The notoriety of MSG goes back a long way. When Chinese restaurants became popular in Britain in the 'sixties, devotees started to notice strange side effects from eating the highly flavoured food. The most obvious were palpitations, dizziness, and headaches which came on within an hour or two of the meal and sometimes lasted until the next day. The cause, it eventually turned out, was this now popular flavour-enhancer, used by the Chinese to heighten the taste of their dishes.

MSG was originally an extract from a Japanese seaweed, though it is now more commonly manufactured from sugar beet, soya beans and wheat. Classed as 'natural', it is now used in many of our meat products. It has no flavour itself, but works by making our taste buds more appreciative of what flavour does exist. The advantages to the food industry are obvious. Rather than pay the price of adding extra lean beef to steak pies, or more liver in pâté, or just putting a bit more meat in the shell of a scotch egg, manufacturers can get away with the legal minimum of meat while making it taste as if they have been generous.

As a result, what became known as 'Chinese restaurant syndrome' can now happen in any British home. You do not have to be addicted to sweet-and-sour prawn balls to over-dose on it. MSG is used in large amounts in so many ordinary products that it is easy to eat a lot of it in one meal without realizing. It is estimated that 6,500 tonnes of flavour enhancers went into food in Britain in 1985, and the bulk of that was MSG. Not only does Britain allow it to be used, there is not even an upper limit on how much can be used. Many ingredients listings show it immediately after the main ingredients and before the other additives, revealing that it is a surprisingly weighty addition.

If you have young children it is worth checking for MSG since it is banned from infant food on the grounds that younger nervous systems simply cannot cope with it. Yet how many mothers never feed their toddlers on sausages, luncheon meat or canned mince, all of which could contain it?

You will not find MSG in most other European countries. Like Red 2G, Britain has taken advantage of a special dispensation to continue using MSG despite its EEC status as a non-approved additive. That is why you may see it labelled as 621, without the 'E'. The Scientific Committee is in the middle of reviewing the evidence, but many countries are against allowing the use of MSG because they feel it could lead to a lowering of food standards.

One piece of research the committee will almost certainly consider appears to show that MSG may cause harm to the embryo in pregnant animals. This serious charge against the chemical has not been backed up with any further research, but it must have the ring of possibility for all those who are frequently affected by MSG. How can a chemical have such widespread and distressing effects in the short term yet do us no harm in the long term?

Nitrites

This last member of the trio is the only one that serves a vital function. Nitrites are always classed as preservatives, though they do add to the colour and flavour of meat products, too. By law, they may be used only in processed cheese and cured meat, such as bacon, gammon or ham, where their purpose is to kill off all the harmful food poisoning bacteria.

Unfortunately, they are also one of the additives most under suspicion, and if it were not for their usefulness, they might well have been banned by now. Nitrites can turn into dangerous chemicals called nitrosamines in some circumstances, and nitrosamines are known to be a prominent cause of cancer in animals. Unlike much of the evidence against additives, very few scientists would dispute the hazards of nitrosamines. Time and again when laboratory animals have been fed small amounts of these substances they have quickly developed tumours, especially of the liver and oesophagus. As yet there is no certain evidence that nitrosamines have the same effect on man, though this must be due in part to the obvious difficulty of devising any conclusive test. However, a related 'nitroso' compound found in cigarette smoke has been shown to cause cancer in man.

Some strange effects have been noticed in people who eat a great deal of cured meat. In Iceland doctors were puzzled for years by the apparently inexplicable phenomenon that a high proportion of diabetic children was born each October. It could not be explained by the occurrence of any known disease, and it happened annually. Finally researchers noticed that in the first two weeks of January each year, when the children were conceived, Icelanders traditionally eat large amounts of smoked, cured mutton. The meat was found to contain nitrosamines, probably encouraged to develop from the nitrites by the smoking process. When the researchers fed mice with the mutton they found that 10 per cent of their offspring became diabetic. The explanation lies in the fact that the nitrosamines cause mutations in the egg and sperm which are passed on to the embryo as defects in the cells of the pancreas. Since the pancreas is responsible for making insulin, the defect results in diabetes.

Scientists have shown that nitrosamines are sometimes present in all sorts of cured meats when nitrites have been used, whether or not the meat has also been smoked. They are the result of a chemical reaction, possibly triggered by bacterial action in the meat. But what is more worrying is that small amounts of nitrosamines may be made in our stomachs after we have eaten nitrites, the temperature, acidity and bacterial action all encouraging their formation.

Meat products are not our only source of nitrites. The 'parent' substance, nitr*ate*, is present in nearly everything we eat, since it occurs naturally in soil and water. Some manufacturers use nitrates and nitrites together in their curing solution. Again, it is possible that our stomach juices may break down this nitrate to nitrite, and so to the harmful nitrosamines.

Traditionally, meat was always cured with nitrate, better known as saltpetre. The Romans discovered that if they rubbed pork with this naturally occurring mineral salt the meat would look an attractive shade of pink, have more flavour and keep for longer. They brought the idea to England, where in medieval times it developed into a pickling cure. The ham or bacon would be soaked in a brine made of salt and saltpetre, then dried and salted. Eventually, at the turn of this century, nitrite was developed from nitrate, and by the Second World War it was commonly used as the main ingredient in the brine.

Apart from the risk of cancer, nitrites are unpleasant substances. Eaten in large amounts they are toxic to man, and particularly to children. Half a teaspoonful is thought to be enough to kill. They produce a condition called methemoglobinemia, in which the blood cannot transport oxygen to the cells and the patient dies of suffocation. In September 1983 a 3-year-old girl from Chesterfield, Derbyshire, found some crumbs of sodium nitrite and licked them. The chemical had been stolen from a local factory and sprinkled round a garage as a weedkiller. A few hours later she was dead. Her blood had turned chocolate brown and bubbled as it became saturated with oxygen which it could not pass on to the cells.

Adults, too, may die from ingesting nitrites, though an accidental dose is more likely to produce vomiting, collapse, and possibly coma. One alarming report from an American researcher suggested that nitrites could even be toxic if we ate a lot of cured meat. Between 3 and 6 lbs in one sitting was estimated to be enough for a potentially fatal dose.

Apart from being certainly toxic and a possible cause of cancer, nitrites also cause sensitive reactions. Usually one of the first additives to be put under the spotlight when parents try to find the cause of a child's allergy or hyperactivity, they frequently turn out to be the guilty party.

It is estimated that the meat processing industry spends £40,000 a year on buying 150 tonnes of sodium nitrite, the main curing nitrite. With so much evidence mounting up against nitrites, it comes as some surprise to discover they are so widely used. In Europe and the US they are still permitted as preservatives, in the absence of an acceptable alternative. Their official designation is E250 (sodium nitrite) and E251 (sodium nitrate). But there are maximum limits for their use, and in Britain these were lowered in 1982 as the first wave of evidence of their link with cancer hit home.

Although industry hotly denies this, there is one group of chemicals which could be used in place of nitrites. Ascorbates, particularly vitamin C or ascorbic acid, are effective preservatives and could do the job of killing off dangerous bacteria in meat just as well as nitrites. But industry refuses to consider them since they would not keep up appearances quite as well as nitrites. Over time, ascorbic acid would allow bacon and ham to lose its rosy colour and its flavour, and that, of course, would mean manufacturers might lose our custom. So far, governments have sided with the industry's view that traditional products must not be changed for the sake of a few scientists' doubts about their safety.

Other additives

All sorts of other little extras go into meat products to make them tastier, prettier and longer-lasting. Uncured products generally contain some alternative type of preservative, usually one of the sulphites (E221–E223) and often sodium metabisulphite. This is bad news for asthma sufferers, who are advised to avoid the sulphites because they can bring on an attack.

Manufacturers love preservatives since they enable them to produce food which does not have to be rushed to the supermarket, and which can hang around on the shelves and in the cabinets for days, or even weeks. As we have seen, they are often cited as an example of how vital additives are.

Ironically, the main preoccupation of food manufacturers is the bacterial safety of their product rather than the long-term implications of producing so many foods with additives. We would not want manufacturers to ignore food-poisoning risks. Dozens of people die each year after eating contaminated food. But while selling meat that is riddled with salmonella or botulism is against the law and could result in a financially crippling case against the maker, selling meat that contains potentially harmful additives has the blessing of the state. Even if an asthmatic were to die, say, from an attack brought on by eating a meat product laced with one of the sulphites, the manufacturer would have nothing to fear.

The sulphites and sulphur dioxide are found in any number of meat products. They are listed on the wrappers of sausages, pies, beefburgers, meat loaf, breadcrumbed meat products . . . the list is endless. But the fact is that not all these preservatives are necessary. Some butchers have already left them out of their recipes for sausages, pâtés and pies since they have the advantage of being able to make their meat products on the premises and sell them the next day. One butcher rang in to a Jimmy Young radio phone-in on additives to explain how he had managed to cut out colour and sulphites: 'As a family butcher, I'm conscious of the need to sell food as pure as possible. I make sausages for my family business, and a proportion of these are free from additives and preservatives. They don't look so appealing and bright as those with preservatives and colour but they are the same price,' he said.

A few unscrupulous butchers have been going to the other extreme and illegally adding sulphur dioxide to their fresh meat to make it last longer and look brighter. When meat has been freshly cut or minced it is bright red because of a reaction between the oxygen in the air and the meat juices. They form a product on the surface of the meat called oxymyoglobin. But after a few hours the colour darkens to a shade of maroon. Although there is probably little difference in its freshness, customers will avoid it. So some butchers have been using sulphur dioxide as a treatment for red-meat joints and mince to keep it looking bright and attractive. But any addition to fresh meat is illegal. Not only could it mislead us about the quality of the meat, it could be dangerous to some people.

One little girl was allergic to preservatives, and so, to avoid them, her parents bought only fresh meat for her to eat. But their careful shopping did not always work, because occasionally she would have an outbreak of the symptoms for no apparent reason. Preservatives can cause gastric irritation, skin rashes and breathing problems. Finally, her father realized that her allergy recurred only after she had eaten mince, which was bought from a butcher's stall in the local market in Leeds. He reported this to the trading standards office, which tested the meat. A few weeks later the butcher pleaded guilty to adding sulphur dioxide to his meat and was fined £200.

Another secret additive is the gas used by some supermarkets when wrapping fresh meat. Carbon monoxide may be used to keep meat looking the right, bright, shade of red inside the plastic film. It works on the surface of the joint by forming a substance called carboxymyoglobin, which looks the same colour as oxymyoglobin, but has the advantage of lasting indefinitely. It is not illegal, but the Food Standards Committee of the Ministry of Agriculture condemns the practice and has recommended that it should not be permitted.

Anti-oxidants are often added to meat products as a form of preservative. They stop the fats in sausages, ham, luncheon meat, bacon, pies and burgers from becoming rancid. That is the reason usually given for their existence, although they are also there to stop other additives from deteriorating! At last, manufacturers are beginning to admit that they are not always necessary.

Meat products generally contain additives in the range E300–E307, vitamin C and similar, but synthetic, substances. They have a reasonable health record with no problems officially recorded. But many doctors believe they may bring on migraines in susceptible people. Many supermarkets feel it is a step in the right direction to remove them from as many products as possible. Cynics have observed that this is not on the grounds of erring on the safe side, but simply because most of these anti-oxidants are synthetic, and so bar a company from using that recently introduced marketing device, the 'no artificial additives' label (see next section).

People who deal with allergy sufferers are more worried about anti-oxidants than the authorities. They have recorded numerous instances in which they are inexplicably linked with migraine, particularly the anti-oxidants known as BHA and BHT (E320 and E321). One of the most puzzling stories involved the anti-oxidants used in sausages, in a case that occurred in Worthing, West Sussex.

The mother of an 11-year-old child named Diana discovered she was allergic to anti-oxidants. 'We were having my version of hot-dogs for tea, but two hours after eating this ordinary sausage Diana was violently ill,' said her mother, Bebe. 'She's now 13 and in the last two years we've discovered that it is only anti-oxidants that affect her. If she eats anything containing them she'll feel dizzy, start vomiting, her vision goes haywire and she comes out in hot and cold sweats. Now she avoids meat products, for obvious reasons.' Both Diana and her younger brother are deaf, and her mum believes the allergy and deafness may be linked. 'I was trying to puzzle out why Diana should be sensitive to anti-oxidants particularly, and then I remembered that during my pregnancies I had an enormously strong craving for crisps. I ate tons of them, mostly the plain flavour.'

Although some crisp manufacturers have now changed their recipes, in the past crisps used to be loaded with anti-oxidants. Diana's doctor, the allergy specialist John Lestor, believes many parents may unwittingly be passing on allergies to their children through eating certain foods around the time of conception and during pregnancy. He is determined that the matter should be officially investigated, but at present his numerous letters to the Ministry of Agriculture have provoked no firm expression of interest.

Polyphosphates are not only among the most iniquitous food additives, especially when they provide the means for manufacturers to defraud the customer, but may possibly be affecting the health of those who eat them in large quantities. Research in France has suggested that certain polyphosphates might upset the digestion by interfering with the necessary enzymes. However, most of the studies done so far show no connection between polyphosphates and long-term health problems such as cancer. That is not to say we should not be concerned about their use. Workers dislike using polyphosphates in the factory because they are known to cause physical reactions. Employees of a firm which makes seasoning mixtures for sausages get severe nose bleeds each time they blend phosphates into the mix. The powdered chemical is tipped from a bag into the machine and inevitably the air becomes thick with phosphate dust. Though extractor fans have been installed to remove the dust as it rises, they are ineffective because they are located in the wrong positions.

You would expect that in the interests of everyone's health hazards of this nature would be investigated. But, amazingly, very little is known about the strange effects some additives can have on the people who have to work with them. While millions of pounds are spent on investigating the results of feeding rats and mice with additives, the health problems suffered by workers have largely been ignored. No one would want workers to act as guinea pigs for the nation's well-being, but if some effort were to be re-directed into studying ailments which are well-known by workers to be connected with a specific food additive, we might all benefit.

Polyphosphates must be prime targets for such investigations. Factory workers who handle polyphosphates have voiced fears that they cause warts. In one chicken plant where polyphosphates are injected into the birds, the men have noticed that an unusually high number of them have warts between the fingers. At an entirely different factory which operates the same process workers have noticed the same problem. And when, during another interview that formed part of the research for this book, warts were mentioned to a health and safety representative who works with polyphosphates at a third factory she said, with great surprise, that she had just noticed a wart on her own hand.

Probably the least understood of all the colours, caramel is neither totally natural, nor totally proven to be safe. Some tests have shown that certain forms of caramel can damage cell tissue and may be a cause of cancer. Others have given it a clean bill of health. Various government and EEC committees are still considering which is right. At the moment it is approved by the EEC, although it is blacklisted by the Hyperactive Children's Support Group, which has established that it may affect sensitive children.

As an additive, caramel has nothing to do with the sweet-smelling liquid we boiled up as children to make toffee. Nowadays various caramel-type substances can be produced synthetically by mixing potent chemicals, like ammonia, with some form of carbohydrate. The resulting bitter brown dye goes into a huge amount of food in great quantities. Astonishingly, caramels make up 98 per cent of all the colours used in food. They are particularly popular in meat pies, canned stews and meat-in-gravy dishes because they simulate that rich, brown, meat-extract colour so well.

From dozens of different types of caramel, the Food Advisory Committee has narrowed down the range to six which manufacturers may use for colouring and flavouring. But in doing so, back in 1979, they realized they had very little safety data on the six forms, and called for research to be done within the year. Research was not completed until many years later and the Committee has still not published either the results or its opinions on the likely safety of caramels. Not until the end of 1986, when the Committee's long-awaited review of food colours is due for publication will we be able to find out just how safe or otherwise these widely used chemicals are.

The EEC's Scientific Committee for Food is in much the same position, although it does not expect to complete its study of caramels until December 1987. While this committee is satisfied that the results so far show no cause for anxiety, it is aware that there is still more research to be done. But it has discovered one very awkward problem in setting safe levels of use for caramels: they are eaten in such large amounts by human beings that it is impossible to get rats to eat enough for the researchers to work out an ADI – acceptable daily intake.

The manufacturers insist they are quite safe. 'We have now supplied the legislators with enough data to show that caramels are neither mutagenic or carcinogenic,' said Alan Carrier of the caramel-making firm CPC. 'We are confident they will get a clean bill of health. As for allergies, we have never seen any positive evidence that proves caramels are a cause of sensitive reactions.'

One worry which has yet to be answered is that many of us could be taking in far more caramel than might be good for us. The EEC's Scientific Committee has laid down a maximum safety limit for caramels but in 1979 the Food Additives and Contaminants Committee (the predecessor of the Food Advisory Committee) admitted in its report that many of us could easily exceed that limit if our diet includes beer, soft drinks and just an average range of foods.

Manufacturers insist they need caramels to put back the

colour lost in processing. 'We must have uniformity,' said one food technologist for a large firm. 'Batches often vary slightly in their colour so we use caramel to darken the gravy colour in all of them so that they'll all be the same.'

However, generous helpings of caramel also come in very useful when a manufacturer tries to pass off texturized gristle and fat (as discussed in the next chapter) as real meat. Even the Chemical Industries Association (CIA) admits that 'if food doesn't look right, it doesn't taste right'. If it were not for caramel, the flaked and reformed lumps of 'trimmings' would look grey and unappetizing. With flavour enhancers, and perhaps extra flavourings too, we will never know that our meat pie contained not one chunk of prime steak, or that our canned stew was entirely lacking in best beef.

If you want to know whether the meat product you are about to buy has been 'beefed up', take a look at its contents list. The chances are that you will not even have to remember the E number. Manufacturers can choose whether to list a colour by number or by name, and most would rather own up to the existence of caramel by using its pleasant-sounding name. The word also sounds far more natural than E150, its official EEC code.

Unlike Red 2G, caramel is classed as a natural colour despite its added chemicals, because the synthetically produced forms are based on exactly the same substance we make when boiling sugar. Some firms capitalize on this fact by labelling their products with such bold phrases as 'no artificial additives', or 'made only with natural ingredients'. To some consumers, this sort of statement implies that no additives have been used at all. In fact the term 'natural' in relation to additives is very misleading: its definition urgently needs revising (see pages 90–2).

Even the caramel makers do not regard their product as natural. They admit there is a need for a new category of additive which is neither wholly natural nor wholly artificial. But the shops and food firms are determined to cash in on the new craze for natural foods for as long as they can, even if it means ignoring the facts. According to CPC, many of the companies it supplies have been asking for advice on labelling, but they have not liked what they have heard.

'Manufacturers have been consulting us because they may have dropped a lot of artificial additives in order to label their food as natural,' said Alan Carrier. 'They want us to confirm that caramel is natural but we have to tell them that that is not our interpretation. It is a manufactured colour produced with a chemical addition. But as far as they are concerned, they prefer to use the word "natural".' This is a point worth remembering if you are swayed by the 'natural' labels.

The only other additives likely to be found in meat products are extra colours and flavours. Tartrazine is sometimes added to sausages in addition to the red dye in order to intensify the colour. The effect it produces is rather similar to the colour of tomato sausages, but with the outcry about tartrazine the practice is dying out. It is still a popular colour for scotch eggs and other breadcrumbed meat products, and may be found in curried meats too. E102, tartrazine's official number, is probably the best-known food colour, although its notoriety is not altogether justified.

This yellow colour, most often associated with squashes and sweets, is known to make sensitive children hyperactive, give them sleepless nights and cause rashes. Susceptible people also find it may cause hay fever, blurred vision and breathing problems. But there is no evidence that it may be the possible cause of longer-term health problems.

Flavours are ubiquitous. Out of 3,500 additives, 3,000 of them are flavourings and about half are synthetic. One of the most popular, significantly, is 'meat' flavour, which is made synthetically from hydrolyzed vegetable protein.

They pop up as ingredients in sausages, hams, canned meats and speciality products (like tandoori chicken) and we think little of them. Yet flavours are often used to compensate for the lack of an expensive ingredient or a costly process. If a manufacturer does not want to go to the expense of wood-smoking his ham, for instance, he can ask his chemist to concoct a mixture which will taste just the same. Only by scrutinizing the pack will we spot the fake which masquerades as the genuine article.

The market for flavourings within the meat industry is currently enjoying a huge growth. Exhibitions are suddenly overflowing with companies wanting to advertise their chemical flavours to the trade. They can produce anything from 'light-roasted beef' to 'chilli con carne' flavour. And if it is not on their lists, they will make it to order. One glossy trade brochure promises that if a manufacturer cannot find what he wants on the company's (very long) list of products it will 'modify in trials in order to accommodate customers' specific requirements'.

The science of flavourings has now become so sophisticated that the boffins can produce minute differences of taste – from lightly roasted pork to full-roasted, and from stewed chicken to fried. The basis for these flavours are slaughterhouse bones, yeast extract, and often synthesized vegetable protein, which, according to one manufacturer, 'give highly potent meat-like flavours, particularly clean and specific in their effect'. The same manufacturer gives us an illuminating insight into the thinking of the food manufacturer when considering which flavours to use. It states in its brochure that its products 'add a mouthfeel and body to foods which is both natural and introduces an element of "home-made" quality'. It makes you wonder how many so-called 'home-made' products are hiding these factory-made flavourings.

Even butchers are about to get in on the flavour bonanza. At least two new companies are promoting the idea of flavoured coatings for fresh meat. Chicken drumsticks can be dipped in powdered curry flavour, spare ribs in 'Chinese' flavour, pork in sweet-and-sour flavour, and these prettily coloured meats make eye-catching displays in the shop window. For the cost of a little bit of flavoured powder, butchers can roll in the profits by adding huge mark-ups to the usual price of their cuts. Chicken legs, for example, which the butcher might sell at £1.20 per lb, can suddenly be sold for £1.80 per lb. One flavouring company tells butchers of their 'four simple steps to increase profits' while another advised them at a recent trade demonstration, 'Flavourings are one of the best things ever to hit a butcher's bank account'.

Unless the labelling is clear, many people are bound to assume that sweet-and-sour pork, or curried chicken, bought from the friendly local butcher, has been made in the same way as at home, with natural ingredients. Not only may flavours mislead us, they are unlike any other major category of additive. They do not have to be approved, and in some cases have never been fully safety-tested. That is why they are rarely listed by their chemical name and do not have an E number. The food industry has argued that there are so many flavourings that it would be a Herculean task to establish a numbering system. The government appears to have been swayed by their arguments, since it has no plans to codify, or call for safety checks, on this gigantic loophole in our food laws.

Natural marketing

As criticism mounted over the use of additives, food companies agonized over their sales figures. What would they do if we all turned against processed food? But the marketing men soon had the answer. They could capitalize on public concern by making changes to ingredients – sometimes quite minor changes – and promoting the results with banner headlines stating 'free from artificial additives'. Whatever the motives, the customer was the winner.

1986 was the year that saw one word – 'natural' – set the cash tills ringing all over Britain. The supermarkets started it, a reflection of their closeness to the concerns of their customers. But not many months after they had set the ball rolling, food companies such as Birds Eye joined in. Firms such as Safeway and Sainsbuiry deserve much credit for their prompt and genuine reaction to the anxieties of their customers.

The 'natural' bandwagon reached ludicrous heights in April 1986 when a poultry-producer launched his brand of whole, roast chicken on to the market with an 'additive-free' tag. The press release referred to it as a 'brand new "health" chicken' and announced proudly that it had been 'naturally roasted'. In fact this wonder chicken had salt, dextrose and sugar on the ingredients list – which presumably did not count as additives in the marketing man's mind. But the fact that anyone selling something as basic as a whole roast chicken has to crow that it does not contain loads of chemical additives shows the appalling state the rest of our food industry had reached.

Meat products have come under scrutiny, and flavour enhancers and anti-oxidants have been some of the first additives to go from a few supermarket 'own-label' ranges. Colours have been more difficult to dislodge. While some foods, such as instant desserts, soft drinks and canned vegetables, appeared to change from artificial to natural colours overnight, Red 2G has stayed put in many manufactured meats. But on pies, pasties, canned meats and 'grill' products the catchpenny phrases 'no artificial additives' and 'made from natural ingredients' have started to appear.

The problem is that our trading watchdogs have no means of checking that all the 'natural' claims are actually true. Public analysts do not have the technical facilities to identify the difference between natural and artificial versions of some additives. This is causing headaches in trading standards departments whose duty it is to check the validity of sales claims like these. 'There's a great deal of money in being able to put a "natural" label on food at the moment, and the temptation must be for some unscrupulous companies to bend the rules,' said Roger Manley, chief trading standards officer for Cheshire. 'We have a major problem at the sampling stage because for some additives we have no way of telling whether they are natural or artificial. The quantities used are often too small to run checks and in many cases we simply don't have the techniques.'

There is no doubt that some of the foods labelled 'natural' are genuinely healthier, and are to be welcomed. But it is worth remembering that many of these products have not necessarily lost their extra colours and flavours altogether;

they may simply have been replaced with naturally derived colour and flavour. And while this looks like good news for consumers, some 'natural' additives are not what they seem.

Apart from caramel, all sorts of colours have been derived from plant sources and are currently entitled to the description 'natural', yet they are hardly what we would *naturally* choose to eat. For example, one yellow colour is being tipped to take over from the artificial dye tartrazine, which is being shunned by increasing numbers of consumers. The new yellow is called crocin, which many are hailing as the answer to the food manufacturers' prayers. The reason for their jubilation? Simply that it can be labelled 'natural'. In fact, it is an extract from the stamens of crocuses which produces the strong yellow colour we may soon be finding in our squash and custard . . . not to mention sausages, scotch eggs or pork grills.

Cochineal, although a traditional kitchen colouring, is generally made from the dried body of a tiny South American insect, although it can also be extracted from egg yolks. Yet it is predicted that this will become a favourite with meat-product makers who want to say their food is natural but cannot bear to drop the extra colour altogether.

Just being natural does not make an additive safe. After all, arsenic is natural! Many of the so-called natural colours have been linked with hyperactivity and sensitivity problems in just the same way as the artificial dyes. And because their colour is invariably weaker than that of many of the artificial alternatives, manufacturers have to add 10–50 times more to get the same effect.

Yet they have never had to go through any official safety tests, or be approved, before they could be used. The government's Food Advisory Committee is aware of the loopholes but as yet has made no suggestion for improving the situation. It is to be hoped that when its long-awaited report on colourings is published at the end of 1986 it will have devised a way which will at least bring natural colours within the framework of safety testing and the law.

The accidental additives

Not all chemicals are added to meat deliberately. Some find their way into what we eat by accident. But they are no less worrying. Between 1980 and 1982 research in the US and Sweden suggested that the chemicals in PVC clingfilm might be harming our health. Amazingly, the substances that give the film its clinginess can migrate and be absorbed by the food they are touching. Research in Britain has shown that up to 50 per cent of these 'plasticizers' in the film may find their way into what we eat. And the problem is worse when they are used to wrap fatty foods. Four years later we are still none the wiser as to whether the American and Swedish researchers' findings were correct.

The scientific studies suddenly hit the headlines in Britain in the summer of 1985. West Midlands Consumer Services Department was quick to put a selection of brands of clingfilm to the test, and its report, in January 1986, stated: 'Initial research shows that plasticizers are much more likely to transfer into fatty foods such as cheese and pork. Temperature also makes an important difference, with more plasticizer being recorded at higher temperatures. Remember, the longer food is wrapped, the higher the level of migration.'

Up until January 1986, the food-wrapping films available in Britain were all of PVC (polyvinyl chloride), which could only be made with plasticizers. Very quickly manufacturers brought out new versions made with plastics such as polyethelene which do not need additives to make them cling. They are now appearing on shop shelves, giving us an alternative way of wrapping food and enabling us to avoid eating plasticizers.

However, most supermarkets still use PVC film to wrap their fresh meat and some meat products, and since many of these foods may stay wrapped for a week or more, a high percentage of plasticizers must be absorbed. But makers of alternative films say the supermarkets are not interested in changing. According to Eric Sabatini, public relations officer for one of the makers: 'They have done tests but as yet no one has moved over to any of the non-PVC films. There seems to be only one reason for their hesitation, and that's the stretchiness of our type of film. If customers prod a chicken, for instance, through the film, it will stretch and leave a mark. So the stores are worried that they could be left with those chickens or joints that have been well prodded. Independent butchers, though, seem to be very aware of the public concern and they have been buying a lot of this type of film.'

Other countries have already put restrictions on the use of PVC films following the US research. Sweden, Belgium, and the Netherlands have brought in regulations limiting the use of plasticizers in clingfilm. West Germany and Italy have banned certain types of clingfilm for use on fatty foods. In Switzerland the government is considering tightening the law, and one huge Swiss supermarket chain has already outlawed PVC film for wrapping any meat, charcuterie, cheese or fish. But in Britain we have no restrictions. As soon as the publicity about the possible dangers of film reached Britain in the summer of 1985 the Ministry of Agriculture was quick to announce a safety study. Its concern about our health was touching. It clearly intended to do its utmost to ensure we should not be allowed to take risks any longer than necessary, so the research was to be rushed through. The committee is due to publish its findings by . . . the spring of 1987.

6

The fat of the land

The laborious progress of the Ministry of Agriculture has affected the issue of fat in our diet as well as other food-related matters. For years, nutritionists have been urging the government to take action which would encourage all of us to eat less fat, for the sake of our health. Only now has a glimmer of light appeared on the horizon as the Ministry draws up plans to make all food manufacturers label the fat in their products.

Nothing has caused more raised hackles in the meat world than the subject of fat. Farmers have been attacked for making money out of it, butchers have been condemned for giving us too much of it, and meat product manufacturers have been accused of disguising it and passing it off as lean meat.

Scientists have shown beyond reasonable doubt that fat and heart disease are linked. In terms of deaths, coronary heart disease is the twentieth century's equivalent of the plague. Three out of ten men and two out of ten women die painfully and often suddenly because of it. Many of them are in their prime and leave behind families with young children. Britain has the tragic honour to top the world league table of premature deaths from heart disease.

Our national diet, rich in fats, stands accused. In the dock are the food producers who profit by our unhealthy tastes. But under greatest fire from the public gallery is the meat industry, which sells so much of this heart-stopping commodity.

Yet in some respects meat has been unfairly singled out for condemnation. It is not quite the 'baddie' we have been led to believe. But the people whose work revolves around producing and selling it have handled its defence clumsily.

In response to the onslaught of criticism, the meat trade, never noted for its easy-going relations with the media, has counter-attacked. Some members of the trade have accused journalists of twisting facts for sensationalism, some have scoffed at the attempts of food writers to expose scandal in the industry, and even the trade's ruling body has threatened action against television programmes which quite rightly questioned the healthiness of meat products.

Farmers too, seem to have an uncanny knack for losing public sympathy when defending their cause. One of the most astonishing defences recently was from a West Country farmer who wrote to the press to disagree with the findings of the COMA report and a booklet published by the Health Education Council. He said, 'Livestock farmers must expose the muddled misconceptions upheld by COMA and summon up full energies to fight the worthless publication *Eating for a Healthier Heart* that circulates among the public, purveying scandal and perpetuating further consumer confusion. This is a so-called "brain-child" publication of a few fossilized specialists that is successfully discrediting the entire livestock industry without any solid evidence.' And the farmer looked forward to the day when he could 'once again market traditional "pure" saturated-fat products to the consumer'.

The antagonism to the press felt by many farmers and butchers is echoed by their trade associations. A leading member of one of these bodies confided to me that he felt meat's adverse television coverage was due to the fact that most of the programme makers were vegetarians! (They are not.) The National Federation of Meat Traders clearly subscribes to the conspiracy theory, too. After no less than five television programmes in one month had criticized meat, the Federation's executive committee said in its annual report for 1985: 'The real effect of these programmes on the consumption of meat and meat products will not be known until the publication of government retail surveys, but the timing of these transmissions led the Committee to wonder whether this was an orchestrated campaign against the food industry in general and the meat industry in particular.'

The Meat and Livestock Commission went one step further by threatening formal action against the programme makers. But the only action taken was against a Granada news report in which it was claimed that the MLC had declined to participate. The MLC insisted that 'declined' was misleading. The invitation had come too late, it said, for a spokesman to be provided.

In the aftermath of all this criticism, the MLC joined forces with the Bacon and Meat Manufacturers' Association to get across the message 'Don't Knock the Great British Sausage'. Half-page advertisements were taken out in Sunday newspapers to remind us that sausages are 'wholesome and nutritious', though they did not mention their contribution to fat intake which had been a major point of contention. The advertisement went on to say that the two associations were taking the space 'as a means of correcting the misleading statements made in recent television programmes – statements which one programme has already retracted'. Although the BBC2 programme *Food and Drink* did clarify that eyeballs and snout could not legally be used in a sausage, no other programme retracted any of its statements, nor did they have any intention of so doing.

The head of Dewhurst, Colin Cullimore, said in a speech at the Smithfield Show that one of the programmes had been 'so neat a piece of disinformation', that it would have aroused 'the admiration of Colonel Gaddafi'. And he referred to some of the medical experts who participated as 'biased pedlars of half-truths'.

To the shopper, this type of bitter defence serves only to make spokesmen appear guilty. The meat industry might have gained a better press by admitting that meat, and especially manufactured meat products, do carry a health risk. Had it channelled its efforts into persuading us to eat less fatty meat dishes, and to trim more carefully, the media might have treated it more kindly. But the meat trade spokesmen are walking a tightrope. On the one hand they want to be seen to be helpful to consumers, and to be up to date with modern trends; on the other, they are answerable to their members –

butchers, farmers, wholesalers – who will bring great pressure to bear on anyone who appears to be jeopardizing their interests.

One fascinating insight into the tough world of the meat industry was given by one of the heads of the trade organizations, who will for obvious reasons remain anonymous. He said: 'Having studied the evidence I do think that households who eat a lot of meat should cut down. How you cook it is important. You should grill rather than fry, drain away the fat and trim anything remaining on the plate. Fresh lean meat is not such a problem, but some meat products are full of fat and people ought to be told to cut down or cut them out. I think eating meat four times a week is a good average, but whatever you do don't quote me on that or my members will kill me. I'd be attacking their livelihood.'

The vegetarian factor

Fanning the flames of the argument has been the Vegetarian Society, which has delighted in the sight of the meat industry squirming beneath the evidence from health experts. The Society has kept up a steady bombardment of press releases to local and national newspapers. In fact, at the height of the health debate in 1984–5 scarcely a month went by without another missive arriving on the nation's news desks.

Unfortunately, in its enthusiasm to turn us all against meat it has not always got its facts straight. For example, one important statement released to the press in September 1984 under the heading 'Bloodshed' claimed that 'medical nutritionists are now recommending a cut of a quarter in meat consumption as a solution to some of the nation's ills'. Since the COMA report had been published just a month before and had mentioned a cut of 25 per cent, you could be forgiven for thinking that the government-backed COMA team must have recommended we cut back heavily on meat. In fact, COMA had recommended a 25 per cent cut in our consumption of *fat*, not meat, which is a very different thing.

However, when challenged, the Vegetarian Society said it

had based this claim on a paper published in *The Lancet* nine months earlier in which nutritionist Caroline Walker discussed the work of another health committee, NACNE (National Advisory Committee on Nutrition Education). The report of the NACNE committee had gone further than COMA and recommended a cut of 25 per cent in *saturated* fat consumption. This was mentioned in the article, but it was still not a recommendation to eat 25 per cent less meat. And although Ms Walker drew up a sample diet to show how it was possible to comply with the NACNE message, nowhere did she *recommend* that meat consumption should be reduced by a quarter.

The fat debate has brought with it a confusion of statistics, but nothing has muddled us more than the way the medical men and industry choose to add up the figures. When health committees urge us to eat lower levels of fat, they state them as a percentage of our total energy intake. So the British Medical Association, for instance, recommends that fat should give us no more than 30 per cent of our total calories (in other words, our total energy intake). But when food manufacturers describe the fat content of their products, they invariably tell us the proportion of fat as a percentage of weight. If they are telling us about butter, say, this makes little difference since virtually everything in the pack is calorific. But when they are describing a sausage, a pork chop or a beefburger this can be very misleading.

One 'healthy eating' leaflet from the meat trade shows how a raw pork loin chop has an average fat content of 29.5 per cent. Compared with the recommendation to eat under 30 per cent you might think a chop would just scrape in. But the two figures bear no relation to each other. The raw pork chop may be 50 per cent non-calorific water. Once cooked the water content will be lower, and its fat content as a percentage of energy will be more than 60 per cent.

When presenting information to the public the meat trade, like most food firms, doggedly sticks to a weight percentage when describing fat content. It sounds lower, it is more easily available in reference books, and it has more meaning for the average customer. But that is not to say there are not occasions when the meat men prefer to talk about fat as a percentage of calories – as in one notable speech by a Meat and Livestock Commission spokesman in which he attacked the vegetarian diet because of its high saturated-fat content.

'The Vegetarian Society launched its Cordon Vert cookery courses with a press release that featured an appropriate dish called Brazilian Bake. This dish derived 77 per cent of its calories from fat,' he said. Perhaps if he had told us its fat content as a percentage of weight it might not have sounded so appalling!

Percentage of fat measured by weight, and by total calories, in trimmed cooked meat

	Percentage by weight	Percentage by calories
Topside of beef (roast)	4.4	25
Breast of lamb (roast)	16.6	59
Leg of lamb (roast)	8.1	38
Leg of pork (roast)	6.9	34
Rump steak (grilled)	6.0	32
Lamb chops (grilled)	12.3	50
Pork loin chops (grilled)	10.7	43
Chicken (roast)	5.4	33
Turkey (roast)	2.7	17
Duck (roast)	9.7	46

The government is about to add to the confusion when its proposals for fat labelling become law. Then most foods, including meat, will have to be labelled with their fat content per 100 g – in other words the measurement will be by weight, rather than as a percentage of energy. But it is to be hoped that enough enlightened manufacturers will also tell us the grammes of fat in a whole portion so that we can check our intake by adding up a daily total.

Not content with sniping at the media, the meat industry has even queried the health lobby's recommendations. While it has been careful to say it welcomes the various medical committees' reports, it has questioned whether we all ought to follow the advice. To understand their argument we need to review the basis for the recommendations.

The health debate

There is little doubt that a diet rich in fats can kill. Population studies show that where people eat a lot of fats, and especially saturated fat, they suffer high rates of heart disease. Studies have also firmly linked fats with cancer of the colon and strokes and there is a mass of evidence to suggest that other cancers are fat-related. In the United States, in 1984, after issuing a statement that many cancers are linked to diet, the US Department of Health launched a prevention campaign.

In Britain we have been very slow to acknowledge the build-up of evidence against fat. Admittedly, there is still no absolute and irrefutable proof that fats cause heart disease or cancer. The only way such theories could be proved conclusively would be to hi-jack two identical groups of people for the whole of their lives, feed one group a high-fat diet and the other a low-fat diet, and see who died off the fastest. Clearly such an experiment would never be allowed, even if there were people willing to offer themselves as guinea pigs. The evidence we *do* have consists of numerous research studies, carried out all over the world, which point in the same direction. Fat is almost certainly the culprit in heart disease, and a very likely candidate in many cancers.

Decades of research have provided the scientists with a pretty clear idea of how the link between heart disease and fat operates. The experts agree that people with a high level of cholesterol in their blood have an increased chance of coronary heart disease. And they have shown that cutting down on fat, particularly one type, saturated fat, can lower the cholesterol level and thus lower the risk of a heart attack. In Japan only 7 per cent of men between 40 and 59 have a high level of cholesterol, and the Japanese have a low rate of heart disease. In Finland, where 56 per cent of older men are clogged up with cholesterol, the death rate from heart disease is one of the worst in the world. There is now good reason to think that polyunsaturated fat may have a beneficial role to play in preventing heart disease, while mono-unsaturated fat is regarded for the moment as a neutral factor.

Of the three types of fat – saturated, mono-unsaturated, and polyunsaturated – it is the first which has been most highly implicated in heart disease. But as yet the research on cancers does not appear to show any greater danger from any particular type of fat. And since the link between fat and cancer is still far from proven there is as yet no recommendation to make a change in diet to reduce the chances of becoming a victim of that particular disease.

The advice from medical researchers studying heart disease is that we should cut down particularly on saturated fat. We may, if we choose, eat more essential polyunsaturated fat and so improve the balance between the two – known as the P/S balance – as long as we cut down our total fat consumption. No firm guidance is given as to what we should do about mono-unsaturated, though since our total fat intake must come down it is likely that this will have to fall as well.

The COMA report recommended that for our health we cut down on all fats by 17 per cent, from an average of 104 g a day to 77–87 g a day. We should cut down on saturated fats by 25 per cent from 49 g to 37 g a day. We could eat 9–17 g of polyunsaturated fats a day, a rise for most people, which means that the third variety of fat, mono-unsaturated, may have to decrease a little.

A previous DHSS committee went even further and recommended we cut all fats by a quarter, and saturated fats even more drastically, by almost half. But in the now infamous suppression of that committee, NACNE, these more stringent recommendations were never officially adopted.

But the British Medical Association backed NACNE's findings in a report published in March 1986. Its Board of Science and Education recommends we cut total fats to 72 g a day and saturated fats to 27 g a day.

What the research does not show is that cutting down on fat will lessen the risk of heart disease for *everyone*. Some people are at risk from a heart attack because of some unknown inherited fault in their circulation system. Others may put themselves at risk by heavy smoking, or being overweight, or taking little exercise. But for those whose main reason for being at risk is too much cholesterol, then cutting down on fat will give them a good chance of avoiding an early death.

The catch is that because we do not know who these people are, we are all being advised to cut down on fat, in order to err on the safe side. The meat industry is none too keen on this advice since it can see future sales dropping. In speeches and statements to the press it questions why we should all have to drop our intake of fat for the sake of a few.

In a glossy brochure produced by the Meat and Livestock Commission it says: 'If the non-smoking, exercising, calorie-conscious, careful-eating generally placid individual (with no obvious evidence to suggest inherited susceptibility) enjoys eating meat, has he already lowered his marginal risk of diseases believed to be fat-related to such a point that there is not likely to be any significant benefit in depriving himself of what he really enjoys by entering into further major changes in the pattern of his eating?

'Most recipients of the dietary advice, whether they act on it or not, will never know whether they have done the correct thing.'

This argument is meant to challenge the current wisdom which urges *all* of us to bring our diets into line . . . *just in case*. But if it were transposed to the seat-belt debate, it would mean that none of us need wear a seat belt since only a small percentage would be saved from serious injury by so doing. Just as it is impossible to predict in advance who is going to be involved in a car crash, so it cannot be foretold who is susceptible to heart disease. Cholesterol in the blood may be measured but it would be impractical to do this in the case of every member of the population, and in any case, the operation would not pinpoint those with an inherited risk.

Trimming the fat

We can follow the experts' advice in various ways. For many people, changing over to drinking only skimmed milk would go a long way to meeting the target. Choosing sunflower, soya or corn oil, which are high in polyunsaturates, would help the P/S balance. And for those who do not already do so, trimming the fat off meat will make a big contribution to lowering overall fat intake.

What is not necessary is the wholesale abandoning of red meat in favour of poultry, fish or even total vegetarianism. If meat is trimmed in advance or on the plate it can easily be under 10 per cent fat by weight (35 per cent when measured as a percentage of energy).

Percentage of fat in trimmed and untrimmed meat by weight

	Untrimmed	Trimmed
Topside of beef (roast)	12.0	4.4
Breast of lamb (roast)	37.1	16.6
Leg of lamb (roast)	17.9	8.1
Leg of pork (roast)	19.8	6.9
Rump steak (grilled)	12.1	6.0
Lamb chops (grilled)	29.0	12.3
Pork loin chops (grilled)	24.2	10.7
Chicken (roast)	14.0	5.4
Turkey (roast)	6.5	2.7
Duck (roast)	29.0	9.7

It is more difficult to cut off the intermuscular fat, which we see as little pockets of fat between the meat muscle. Even though we may conscientiously trim off the outer fat margin, if we still eat these small nuggets of fat they can add a few vital percentage points to our intake.

It is still not widely realized how important the leanness of the original carcass is when trying to cut down on fat. Those pockets of fat you see most often in a roast joint, in a chop or a steak are correspondingly bigger when they have come from an animal which has been allowed to grow large and fat. But not only that, the actual fatty acids within that fat tissue are more concentrated. That is why it is so important that the carcass starts off lean, in order to keep the intermuscular fat to a minimum.

There is another very good reason to start fat-trimming on the farm rather than later on in the chain. While farmers continue to produce fat animals, that spare blubber will find a home, and it is most likely to turn up in our meat products, such as sausages and pies. As we will see in Chapter 8, the law says fat *is* meat. If slaughterhouses continue to have volumes of it to spare after they have trimmed their carcasses, then meat manufacturers will buy it, disguise it and sell it to us to eat.

Thanks to a huge publicity drive by the Meat and Livestock Commission, many farmers are now aware of the health hazards of producing fat carcasses. Some have voluntarily made great efforts to breed leaner animals and send them to the slaughterhouse earlier, but they have gained little credit, either publicly or financially. It takes time for a farmer to change his methods, and perhaps his breeding stock, in order to satisfy our need for leaner meat. Such big changes need encouragement, but the government has been appallingly slow to reward their efforts.

Pig farmers have been particularly successful by selectively breeding for leaner animals. In the ten years from 1973 the outer fat thickness has decreased by 25 per cent, from 19 mm to 14 mm. Unlike that for sheep and cattle, the pricing system for pigs directly rewards the farmer for producing a leaner carcass. As a result, we can buy joints of pork which show almost no visible fat.

A few beef farmers have also been trying to produce leaner meat. Rather than using traditional Hereford or Aberdeen Angus bulls to sire beef cattle, a number of farms have turned to continental breeds such as Charolais, Limousin and Simmental, which produce a less fatty animal. Because beef from bulls is a lot leaner than that from steers, some farms have been raising male calves 'entire' – without castration. And although controversial, one beneficial result of using hormones on cattle is that they produce a leaner animal.

As lovers of lamb can testify, sheep farmers have not done so well at producing leaner meat. Less than a quarter of the sheep produced in 1984 could be classed as lean or very lean. Nearly three-quarters were middle to fat. As a result the lamb on our plates is often thickly streaked with fat.

Yet the cattle and sheep farmers who are producing these heart-stopping cuts of meat are being paid handsomely to add to the nation's ill health. EEC bonuses are still being paid on carcasses dripping with fat, so there is little incentive for a farmer who is set in his ways to change. The blame rests with the British government, which controls the payment of the EEC money, known as the variable premium. Rather than leading the way to promoting healthier meat the Ministry men have sat on their plump backsides and left it to farmers to make most of the changes.

When a farmer takes his stock to market he is paid according to the weight of the animals. In a live auction he will be paid so much a kilo for their 'liveweight'. If he sends them direct to the slaughterhouse he will receive an amount per kilo based on their 'deadweight' – without head, feet or hide.

In order to qualify for the variable premium the animals must be of a certain size and shape, though the standards are so simple, very few fail to get the money. The Ministry of Agriculture lays down the classification scale, which is based on carcass size and fatness. It runs from 1 to 5, from lean to very fat. Grades 3 and 4 are split into two subdivisions, L for lean and H for heavy. Sheep farmers must produce animals between 1 and 4L to get the money, cattle farmers are paid the premium on all classes except 5. But cattle and sheep which fall in the 3H and 4 categories are still much too fatty, according to the medical experts.

In July 1984 the COMA report urged the Ministry to

encourage the production of leaner carcasses by adjusting the grading system. At the time only class 5 carcasses were outlawed from the premium scheme for sheep, and 5H for cattle. Eighteen months later a minor adjustment meant that those sheep at the heavy end of category 4 and all class 5 cattle would also lose the premium. But the Ministry's dickering is unlikely to have much effect.

'The Ministry definitely hasn't gone far enough,' says Professor Michael Haines, one of Britain's leading agricultural marketing experts. 'When they excluded 4H it was a very half-hearted measure designed to give them a bit of good publicity. But very few animals fell into that category anyway, so it's unlikely to make a great deal of difference. They should have outlawed the whole of fatclass 4, but they were afraid of the farmers' backlash.'

To a sheep farmer this EEC bonus, known as the variable premium, is the difference between a comfortable living and bankruptcy. The premium adds about a third to the price he gets for his animals. In January 1986, for instance, the slaughterhouse price for sheep was £1.86 per kilo, and the premium added 51.3p per kilo on top. Beef farmers do not rely so heavily on the premium since it adds only about 10 per cent to the price they get for their cattle.

Even so, the variable-premium scheme could be a useful carrot in persuading farmers to produce leaner animals, if only the officials at the Ministry of Agriculture felt as strongly about the nation's diet as our eminent medical nutritionists do.

Flab on the slab

The government is not alone in encouraging farmers to keep up their fatty habits. Many butchers still seek out the plumper carcasses in preference to the lean. Surprisingly, they seem to be even fonder of the fat than farmers. In a survey by the Meat Research Institute only a third of farmers now prefer fatty beef when it is presented to them on a plate. But 50 per cent of butchers are still avoiding the leaner cuts.

Some are enlightened enough to search out leaner carcasses, or to use newer butchery techniques to trim off the fat. During the summer of 1986 the Meat and Livestock Commission persuaded about 100 butchers to join their 'Super Trim' scheme. Worried that if butchers did not keep up with the times we might all start avoiding meat because of its fat, they urged butchers in eight different regions to trim off all the visible fat from the meat on display. Prices were higher, but the overall cost, pound for pound, of a piece of lean meat remained the same.

Many supermarkets have been using modern methods to trim their meat for years. Apart from cutting off the fat, they often try to buy leaner carcasses, preferring to start off with meat from category 2 rather than 3 or 4. According to the Federation of Fresh Meat Wholesalers they 'like to have their cake and eat it'. Most multiple retailers are in such a strong bargaining position they can dictate their terms. 'They want the best grades of meat, from the leaner end of the scale, and they will make the slaughterhouse do the trimming as well,' said Federation spokesman Mark Symons. The problem is, there are never enough carcasses in class 1 and 2 to go round. The bulk of cattle and sheep fall into fatclasses 3 and 4, which is too fatty for most people's taste nowadays.

Nevertheless, it is those medium-to-fatty grades which many butchers look for when they buy from the slaughterhouse or market. Despite evidence to the contrary, many butchers insist that meat will not cook well or taste good without plenty of fat. And they tend to scoff at the health lobby, which has pointed out the dangers of eating too much fat. At the 1985 Smithfield show, I quizzed 15 butchers from around Britain about their attitudes to fat. All insisted that meat needed a good layer of the stuff to cook, all told me lean meat did not have as much flavour as fatty meat, and all but three laughed when I raised health objections.

Even the butchers' trade association insists meat must have a good covering of fat to cook. 'It is widely recognized that fat is a basting medium,' said John Fuller, of the National Federation of Meat Traders. 'If you don't have a useful amount of fat you can end up with a rather dry joint that tastes like shoe leather,' he said.

It is not that butchers are unaware of the fat controversy. They are now so worried about our attitude to fat that they have dreamed up a euphemism to describe it. Rather than talk of a well-fattened animal they now refer to a well-finished beast. One Durham butcher confided, 'The word "fat" is taboo so we say "finish" now. It sounds better.'

Does meat need fat?

The diehard views of some sections of the butchery trade have undoubtedly slowed down the changeover from fat to lean animals on the farm. Yet there is now a mass of scientific evidence which shows they are wrong. Amazing though it may seem, it has been proved that fat does not make any real difference to the taste or texture of meat. And rather than a layer of fat helping the joint to stay juicy, it will actually lead to more cooking losses, not less.

While butchers have been telling us that the fat layer round a joint is vital, and that the thick marbling will help the meat to cook, scientists at the Food Research Institute in Bristol have proved the opposite. At the 1982 Royal Show they asked 700 consumers to taste samples of roast beef from fat and lean animals and to give them marks for flavour, tenderness and juiciness. 'Sixty-six per cent of the consumers found no difference in the samples, 17 per cent gave higher scores to the leaner meat, and 17 per cent gave higher scores to the fatter meat,' said their report. 'In practice even the leanest animals contain sufficient fat for full flavour development.'

The fat makes no difference to tenderness either, even when extremely lean joints are cooked. Another test at the Food Research Institute checked the eating quality of pork which was much leaner than the national average. 'Tenderness, which is the major factor determining overall acceptability, did not differ significantly between the lean and very lean groups,' said Dr Monica Winstanley. 'Hence there appears to be no significant effect of fatness on texture, flavour or juiciness down to fatness levels well below those currently produced for the UK market.'

Most surprising of all are the tests on cooking losses, which show that lean beef with no fat cover loses *less* weight than lean beef with a fat cover. In the slow oven test, for instance, one kilogram of lean beef with no covering of fat shrank to 810 g, while a kilo of lean beef with a 10-mm wrapping of fat shrank to 760 g. This strange difference has nothing to do with the fat dripping away, since the fat cover was weighed separately. 'Interestingly, in both fast and slow ovens, slightly more weight was lost from the lean portion of fat-covered joints, than in lean joints without fat covering,' said the test report.

In the light of this pretty conclusive evidence, we might question the motives of those butchers who still insist on selling us fat. We may be paying lean-meat prices for that unnecessary layer round our joints, steaks and chops, and, what is more, it could be harming our health.

The mince scandal

One of the most common ways of palming unwanted fat off on the consumer is through the mincing machine. Some types of mince may be over 30 per cent fat, and in one of the worst cases, a Leeds butcher was found guilty of putting 42 per cent fat into his product. Worse than that, he had the cheek to call it 'best mince'! The descriptions give very little guidance to quality, as a survey from the Local Authorities Coordinating Body on Trading Standards proved. In 1980 it found the highest percentage of fat in meat marked 'lean mince'. The samples contained an average of 24 per cent fat while meat labelled simply 'mince' had just 20.8 per cent fat.

LACOTS gave its evidence to the government-appointed Food Standards Committee in 1983. It showed that shop-keepers were putting anything from under 5 per cent to over 35 per cent fat in their mince, and pointed out that the consumer had no way of knowing which mince was good value or good for health. Not only were the descriptions a useless guide to quality, but price did not help much either. Expensive mince might be full of fat, while an economical buy might turn out to be lean.

The meat traders, on the other hand, claimed there was no need to control the fat in mince. In their submission to the committee they said customers could judge the fat content of mince by its appearance, and that some people preferred fattier mince for cooking certain dishes. They also claimed that controls would place a heavy burden on the sellers of meat, and could mean price increases.

But the committee disagreed. 'We concluded unanimously that there was a need to introduce specific controls over the composition and labelling of mince. Not only would this provide the purchaser with consistent information about the quality and content of the product, but it would also help remove the disagreement between enforcement authorities and traders . . . on the question of maximum fat content.'

Until now trading standards officers have worked on the basis that mince should be no more than 25 per cent fat, but butchers have not always agreed, and the arguments fought out in the courts have often been heated. Backing the trading watchdogs have been the public analysts, who are responsible for carrying out tests on food. After a national survey in 1976 their association recommended the fat limit should be 25 per cent.

But the Food Standards Committee, when it reported in 1983, did not adopt that approach to the problem. Rather than an upper limit it proposed that butchers should be able to decide the proportion of fat to lean, as long as they then labelled the mince with its fat content. That way the customer would know what he or she was buying, and the system was likely to outlaw very fatty mince simply because few people would choose to buy it. So a butcher who was selling genuinely lean mince could mark it 'not more than 12 per cent fat', while someone who was selling an economy mince could mark it, say, 'not more than 27 per cent fat'.

Three years later we *still* have no way of knowing how much potentially fatal fat we are being sold in our mince. The government has promised to act on the Food Standards Committee's proposals, but its latest suggestion, announced before this book went to press, was nothing short of an attempt to legalize fraud. The Ministry indicated that it was thinking of setting up three categories for mince with maximum fat contents of 15 per cent, 25 per cent and 40 per cent. While 15 per cent is a reasonable maximum for lean mince, and 25 per cent acceptable for ordinary mince, the 40 per cent limit has left trading standards officers incredulous.

If the civil servant who worked out this figure had ever cooked mince with 40 per cent fat, he would know that it can cause disaster in the kitchen. Shepherd's pies bubble over, home-made burgers shrivel, and chilli con carne becomes a greasy mess! Even the worst court cases so far heard on poor-quality mince have rarely involved as much as 40 per cent fat. Magistrates have fined butchers for selling mince with 30–35 per cent fat because they believed even that was not up to standard. If the Ministry goes ahead with this ludicrous proposal it will be giving butchers a licence to lower standards even further.

While butchers may be buying the class 3 and 4 carcasses, manufacturers generally buy up the fattiest carcasses of all. Since the fat in meat products is not obviously visible, they have no good reason to 'super trim' their meat. Far from cutting off the fat, many firms will buy up the fatty trimmings from abattoirs and wholesalers and use it to pad out their products. That is why items such as luncheon meat, salami and sausages tend to be so fatty. Grilled pork sausages may be 24.6 per cent fat by weight (70 per cent of total energy), luncheon meat may be 26.9 per cent fat (77 per cent of energy), and salami may be an astonishing 45.2 per cent fat by weight (83 per cent of energy).

7

And now the good news . . .

There is no doubt that meat has had a raw deal in the health debate, but the fact is that much may be said in its favour. While the meat industry has been busy launching fierce counter-attacks against vegetarians and the press, it has failed to get across some surprising but vital truths about meat.

Meat has acquired an appalling reputation in terms of health. For many people, the very mention of dietary fat conjures up images of forbidden lamb chops, bacon, roast beef and stews. Some of our favourite foods have ceased to be enjoyable because we now carry a burden of guilt for even desiring to eat meat. Meat is regarded as far more of a threat to our health than any other single fatty food.

Yet meat's vastly unhealthy image is largely due to a simple misunderstanding. For years health committees, medical experts and the press have based their advice on a set of government figures which are fatally flawed; these make meat appear to be far more of a danger than it really is.

Since fat was first linked with heart disease, the health lobby has been trying to persuade us to cut down our intake. To help us it has cited the three worst culprits in our diet – dairy products, cooking fats and, of course, meat. As a result millions of us now view our Sunday roast with suspicion – if, indeed, we have not abandoned it altogether.

The figures it gives show that meat and meat products make up just over a quarter of all the fat we eat, butter, margarine and oils make up a third, while milk, cream and cheese represent a fifth. In some reports the categories have been changed around, but the message is the same: meat is one of the fattiest elements in our diet.

A study carried out by the Food Policy Research Unit of

Bradford University showed that 71 per cent of us think meat is the main source of fat in the diet. But in reality meat is not even second in the fat stakes. When the source of the figures is analysed it shows that meat trails in third position behind dairy products (milk, cream, cheese) and fats (butter, margarine, lard, oils).

Meat's bad image stems from the calculation methods used by the Ministry of Agriculture's National Food Survey which is published every autumn, two years in arrears. What has been continuously overlooked is that this is not a survey of what we *eat*, but of what we *buy*. In the case of meat this makes a tremendous difference. While the meat in our shopping basket may add up to a quarter of all the fat we have bought, a large proportion of it will be wasted.

For a start, many cuts of meat will lose part of their fat in the preparation. As braising and stewing steak is chopped up for the pot any lumps of fat and gristle will almost certainly be thrown away. Many people trim bacon and chops of excess fat. In the oven some of the fat will drain off and will be left behind in the baking tray. Even after serving not all the fat will be eaten, for many of us who dislike fat or prefer not to eat it for health reasons will leave trimmings on the side of the plate.

At a conservative estimate, about a third of the meat fat we buy in the high street never gets eaten. Yet it is impossible to separate the fat from the food in the other categories. If we buy a quarter of cheese we either eat it or throw it away. We cannot eat part of it but leave the fat! The same goes for cream, or butter, or lard or oil. The only other food which may have been done a disservice by the government's survey method is milk. Those who buy silver– or gold-top could, if they wished, pour off the cream. But even the dairy companies admit this is unlikely. Consumers who are worried about fat in milk now buy skimmed or semi-skimmed, and these are accounted for in the figures.

So the government statistics are misleading unless they are understood. It would be more accurate to say that meat contributed about 17 per cent of the fat in our diet, and that therefore each of the other categories contributed slightly more.

The problem is that the government figures are the best available. It is virtually impossible to produce national annual statistics on which foods put the most fat into our bodies rather than into our shopping baskets. And of course it must always be remembered that they are averages. There are families who never trim meat, use all the 'juices' in the gravy, and eat everything on the plate. For them the message to be wary of meat is of vital importance. But for all the others who have always trimmed meat by force of habit, or who have recently started to do so, the image of meat as a 'killer' is unnecessarily alarming.

Some individual meat products have gained an atrocious reputation. The very thought of sausages and burgers conjures up visions of fat mountains for many of us. While there is no denying that many manufactured meat products have unhealthy levels of fat, they are by no means the only culprits. 100 grams of quiche (a large wedge) has slightly more fat than 100 grams of sausages (two), yet how many of us would not choose quiche as the 'healthier' alternative for lunch? Plenty of us would think nothing of scoffing a small bag of peanuts with a drink before dinner, but gram for gram those nuts probably contain twice as much fat as the meat we will be eating afterwards, and more than two-thirds as much saturated fat. And naughty nibblers might be astonished to learn that three chocolate biscuits add up to as much fat as a generous beefburger.

Meat was destined to get a bad name as soon as the health experts pointed a finger at animal fats. The very word 'animal' meant it got an unfair share of the blame when, in fact, milk, butter, cream and cheese were just as much implicated. In fact, the phrase 'animal fats' has been used quite wrongly by health experts in place of the more scientific-sounding 'saturated fats'. But the two are not the same. Some vegetable fats, such as palm oil and coconut oil, and some ordinary margarines, are high in the 'baddy' saturates. And there are even meats which have a surprising amount of the 'goody' polyunsaturates, about which more will be said later.

Even the Health Education Council is guilty of such over-simplification. In its booklet *Fat, Who Needs It?* it advises, 'In particular, cut down the solid, mainly *animal* (including *dairy*) fats – "saturated" fats as they are called' (HEC's emphasis). Quite justifiably, many experts have tried to boil down the scientific jargon into a message we can all understand, but meat especially has been the loser.

The Bradford University Research Group noted that this had left many shoppers with a confused idea about which fats they should cut down on. 'The conviction that saturated fat is "Bad for you" and that fat is synonymous with animal fats is widely held,' it observed in 1985. 'In the work reported here both the qualitative and quantitative studies provided evi-

Fat content of meat products versus other foods

	Percentage fat by weight		*Percentage fat by weight*
Corned beef	12.1	Quiche	28.1
Luncheon meat	26.9	Chocolate digestive	24.1
Haggis	21.7	Wafer biscuit	29.9
Salami	45.2	Mince pie	20.7
Frankfurters	25.0	Cheesecake	34.9
Beef sausage (grilled)	17.3	Single cream	21.2
Pork sausage (grilled)	24.6	Double cream	48.2
Saveloy	20.5	Cheddar cheese	33.5
Beefburger (grilled)	15.4	Crisps	35.9
Cornish pastie	20.4	Roasted peanuts	49.0
Pork pie (individual)	27.0	Plain chocolate	29.2

N.B. These figures are based on traditional products checked some years ago and take no account of newer trends for low-fat sausages, dry-roast peanuts, low-fat crisps, etc.

dence to support this assertion. 76 per cent of respondents in
the qualitative study agreed in some degree with the statement "nowadays we are educated not to eat animal fats".'

It comes as some surprise, then, to learn that meat is an
important source of *polyunsaturated* fat, and that certain meat
animals contain more of the desirable polyunsaturates than
they do of the undesirable saturates. In 1983 just over 17 per
cent of the *essential* fat in our diet came from meat. The only
food group to give us more were the margarines and oils,
which many of us buy specifically because of their health-
promoting properties.

These vital polyunsaturates are to be found not in the fat
you can see, but tucked away inside the lean meat tissue.
Scientists have found the cell walls are coated with essential
fats, and they are also contained within the cell itself.
Although amounts are small they are by no means negligible.
According to Dr Hugh Sinclair, one of the country's leading
experts in essential fats, 'Eskimos depend upon meat as a
source of one essential fatty acid which is contained in the cell
membranes. This shows meat is worth thinking about. Essential fatty acids, by their very nature, can't be made by our
bodies or they wouldn't be essential, so anything that supplies
them is important.'

The fat we can see with our eyes – the beneath-the-skin
layer, the intermuscular pockets and the marbling – are
almost wholly saturated and mono-unsaturated fatty acids.
So by trimming meat carefully of its visible fat we are
removing the bad without touching the good. That means we
are not only cutting down our intake of fat, we are also
improving the vital P/S balance. In their raw, untrimmed
state we know that beef and lamb have saturated and
polyunsaturated fat present in a ratio of 10:1. Pork is even
better at 5:1. If the meat is from a lean carcass, and is
trimmed of all visible fat, that ratio could come down
significantly. In other words, by eating more lean meat and
less fat we are doing just what the nutritionist ordered.

Percentage of saturated and polyunsaturated fat in various untrimmed meats

	Saturated	Polyunsaturated
Beef	44.9	4.3
Lamb	52.1	5.0
Pork	42.5	8.3
Chicken	35.1	14.9
Turkey	36.5	29.5
Grouse	24.6	62.2
Partridge	27.6	25.1
Pheasant	35.2	12.8
Rabbit	43.3	34.0

N.B. The remaining percentage of fat in each case is made up of other types of fatty acid, including mono-unsaturated.

Of the most common meats, chicken is a particularly good source of polyunsaturates. It is fairly low in fat, and what fat there is has the saturated and polyunsaturated varieties in a ratio of 2:1. Without the skin, which contains much of the fat, it is likely that you would be left with as much polyunsaturates as saturates. Turkey is even better. Because it has far more flesh to skin its fat content is even lower than that of chicken. Even before trimming there is almost as much polyunsaturated fat as there is saturated, and after removing the skin the polyunsaturated fats actually outweigh the saturates by as much as 2:1.

Although it may come as something of a shock to realize that meat has any polyunsaturated fat at all, it is still by no means enough to give us our full recommended intake. And although it is easy to trim off the visible fat, there are some meats for which this is just not necessary.

Determined meat eaters who really want to eliminate fat as far as possible should try game. All the major supermarkets now offer a selection in their larger stores, with venison and pheasant being particularly popular. Astonishingly, game has almost no fat – and what little there is, is high in polyunsat-urates. Grouse is probably the most amazing bird of all. Roast, it is only 5.3 per cent fat, and that is nearly all polyunsat-urates. Venison, pheasant, partridge, pigeon, quail, hare and rabbit, too, are all good enough to please the nutritionists.

Percentage of fat in game

	Percentage by weight	Percentage by energy
Grouse (roast)	5.3	28
Partridge (roast)	7.2	31
Pheasant (roast)	9.3	39
Pigeon (roast)	13.2	52
Hare (stewed)	8.0	37
Rabbit (stewed)	7.7	39
Venison (roast)	6.4	29

One scientist put it down to all the shivering wild animals do! They have to search for miles to find food and brave freezing temperatures, and they rarely build up much of a fat layer. What fat they do have tends to be high in the essential fats because of their diet. They eat what they can find, and because that is only likely to be natural grasses, seeds and leaves, high in polyunsaturates themselves, their own flesh is similarly high in them. This phenomenon is true for all wild animals – from grouse to giraffe. But if you take them out of their natural habitat, keep them warm and cosy and feed them plenty of commercially mixed food, their fat levels will shoot up and the polyunsaturated content will plunge.

This was shown by Dr Michael Crawford and others in a paper published by the International Journal of Biochemistry in 1970. 'The samples from the zoo-maintained giraffe were analogous to the domestic animals but not the two giraffes of similar age that were taken from Nabiswa, Sebei, in Uganda.

The zoo giraffes were traditionally fed on hay and some concentrates and the wild giraffes had access to a variety of trees including *Acacia* and *Balanites* species. The kernel of the fruit from *Balanites aegyptiaca* studied by us contained 20 per cent of its fresh weight as oil, of which more than 50 per cent was C18:2 (polyunsaturated).'

Our domestic animals, on the other hand, are fed high-carbohydrate diets, get little chance to stretch their legs, and in the intensive rearing houses so popular nowadays the shiver factor does not arise. Small wonder that they are so high in fat, and that compared to that of game animals, their fat is so full of saturates. In effect, our domestic meat-producing animals are now kept too cosy for *our* own good.

According to Dr Crawford, 'It is well known that domestic animals are reared on a high-carbohydrate diet providing a high non-essential-fat-to-protein ration. But it may not have been appreciated that this was different from [that of] other similar mammals. Hence wild carnivores are often thought of as eating a high saturated-fat diet and the same is true of African communities who make use of wild or semi-wild animal products. Our data indicate that where large ruminants are free to select their own food and have not been manipulated genetically other than by 'natural selection' pressures, their muscle lipid composition is different from that of the modern domestic animal. Their muscle tissue lipids reflect the vegetable oils rather than the so-called hard fats which we usually associate with animals.'

It is possible to turn this knowledge to our advantage. While the fat of wild animals will be affected for the worse by a 'domestic' diet, so the fat of domestic animals can be changed for the better by a diet that is already rich in essential fats.

'We know that until 1939 pork was a very good source of polyunsaturates,' said Dr Sinclair. 'Pigs were fed on household waste and were free to roam about grubbing up natural foods like roots. . . . Since then they have been fed increasingly on carbohydrates and the polyunsaturated content of their meat has gone down. But it could easily be increased again for any of our domestic animals simply by changing to a more natural diet.'

The research reflects what many of us have known in our hearts all along. There is a price to be paid for intensive farming and it is not only paid by the animals who suffer the unnatural conditions we impose upon them. All the evidence points to the fact that it may also be damaging our health. When the light finally dawns it could herald a return to old-fashioned ways of farming, at least for some. The day may not be far away when a drive in the country could guarantee the sight of pigs wallowing in the fields.

The fat antidote

While some farmers might go back in time to beat the fat menace, others look set to take a trip into the future. Scientists are experimenting with a most unusual way to keep our meat fat-free. They plan to destroy the fat cells with antibodies, in much the same way as our own immune system destroys foreign intruders.

By injecting the animal when it is still young with this special type of antibody they can call on its own body's defences to attack fat cells as they are formed. With less storage space for fat, food will be converted into muscle, which makes production more cost-effective for the farmers, and more healthy for meat eaters.

So far, experiments on rodents have shown that the method can produce 30 per cent less body fat and correspondingly more flesh, although the tests have not yet been finalized on sheep, pigs and cattle. If those results are true for our meat-producing animals, then an antibody injection will be far more effective in reducing carcass fat than hormones. With the hormone ban agreed by the EEC due to take effect in three years' time, these antibody injections could be the answer to the farmers' prayers. The researchers hope to have their magic potion commercially available by 1989.

The scientists involved are keen to point out that the method does not carry the same risk of dangerous residues as steroid injections. If there were any antibodies remaining in the meat they would be destroyed on cooking, and, in any case, could not survive our digestion process, they say. Of course, some people might like the idea of taking in compounds that could destroy their fat cells! The scientists are already aware that their products could be in enormous demand by slimmers given that they are proven safe and effective for livestock.

8

The inside story

More than any other food, meat has been debased. Its finest points – flavour, texture and nutritional value – have been swept aside by an industry ever greedy for an extra penny profit. Price has been its downfall. We spend more on meat each week than on anything else in our shopping baskets. No other staple food costs so much a pound and yet is such a necessity for the vast majority of the population. Manufacturers, too, have to pay a lot for the meat they transform into such high-value products. So every scrap they can save, every corner they can cut, means money in the bank.

Reflect, for a moment, on what they have done to one of our best-loved meat traditions. Once a plate of roast ham was a delight for the tastebuds. The full rounded flavour came through with each morsel and the texture was firm enough to give your teeth some work to do. It was a satisfying food. The same could never be said of the modern-day packeted slime that, until recently, masqueraded as ham. It tasted of little other than salty water, had the consistency of clingfilm, and slithered down the throat in a most disgusting way.

Ham is the perfect example of what the profit motive has done to a beautiful food. In the beginning there was salt pork. A thousand years before Christ people had discovered how to cure meat. Plain sodium chloride was rubbed into a leg of pork every few days and after months of this treatment the salt would have infiltrated every fibre, preserving it from bacteria. Our ancestors finally discovered they could cut out some of this tedious labour by soaking the pork in a solution of salt and then hanging it until dry. Often the water or salt, or both, was contaminated with nitrates from the soil and they gave the meat a pink colour when cured. Towards the

end of the eighteenth century chemicals called nitrites, der-
ivatives of nitrates, were deliberately encouraged to form in
the brine to help in the curing and preservation. But dry
curing continued, the salts being a mixture of plain sodium
chloride and nitrates, and the results, like genuine York ham,
can still occasionally be found in specialist shops.

Traditionally, to make cooked ham, the cured leg of pork
would be roasted in a dry oven, or sometimes steamed and
roasted. So far so good. Even despite the initial soaking, ham
was still a relatively dry delicacy by the time it was eaten. Up
to this point, most ham was still made in the back kitchen for
the family to feast on through the winter. Then, at the turn of
the century, the cured-meat industry was born.

The entrepreneurs soon invented the injection technique,
which although it was labour-intensive at first, meant the
pork absorbed the curing solution much more quickly. By the
'fifties sophisticated injection machines speeded up the process even further by running a battery of needles through the
flesh. Rather than 80 days, the traditional curing time, the
ham was mature and ready to be cooked after only three
weeks, one week for injection and soaking in the brine and
two weeks for hanging.

By cutting down the time between buying in the pork and
reaping in the profits, the companies had saved a lot of
money. The ham was still very close to the traditional dry
texture, but the changeover to injection-curing heralded the
demise of real ham.

After the first faltering steps, it soon became possible for the
manufacturer to control the amount of solution he injected
into his meat. In the 'sixties needles became finer, machinery
was developed which could cover a joint of pork with tiny
pinpricks, and the solution could be squirted at varying
depths to cover the meat tissues evenly. Whereas in the old
days meat had to be hung to let the salts permeate right
through, now manufacturers could cut down the maturing
time because they knew their injection method had reached
the parts old-fashioned curing could not reach. Again they
could save on time, but, more important, if they steam-cooked

the ham while it was still dripping wet, they could make money out of selling water.

Last but by no means least came the discovery of polyphosphates. These miraculous chemicals could persuade the cells of the meat to swell up and absorb extra liquid. After injection the pork joints were divided into their individual muscles and tumbled in a solution of polyphosphates. Now there was no pretence of taking time to mature the meat. The game was on to see who could make the most money out of a gullible public who were willing to pay ham prices for water, and did not appear to mind that the product was wet and rubbery. The winners were the companies which, by the 1980s, had pushed up injection rates until a third of the final product was unnecessary water. Some were so bad that the liquid could be seen swimming around in the plastic pack. Rather than a natural water content of 60-70 per cent, some ham consisted of 80 per cent water. Had it then been labelled, it would have been not 'ham with added water' but 'water with added ham'!

The adulteration of ham was a slow but relentless process. Traditional dry-cured ham all but disappeared as companies were forced to follow the lead set by the rubber barons. Only some taste-conscious butchers, and a few specialist manufacturers, prevented real ham from dying out altogether.

In the face of this appalling debasement the trading standards service was virtually powerless. Although a few of the most blatant offenders were taken to court, in the main the lowering of standards was too slow, and too subtle, to give it any firm grounds for prosecution. Until July 1986 there was no law which dealt with added water in hams, or in any other meat products. Our trading watchdogs were faced with trying to prove that manufacturers were selling meat which was not 'of the nature, substance or quality demanded' by the customer – a requirement of the Food Act – or that it offended the Trade Descriptions Act. Since most hams in the shops were watery, and we appeared to buy them quite happily, it was often very difficult to convince a court of the former argument. TDA cases tended to be more successful, but could only be taken against firms which had such little regard for the truth that they labelled their plastic ham with phrases such as 'traditional', 'country-style' and 'real farmhouse ham'.

Only the government had the power to prevent real ham from becoming a thing of the past. But despite numerous warnings its actions came too late and were too weak to turn the clock back. Although it has probably stopped the worst excesses, the new Meat Product Regulations which came into force on 1 July 1986 have simply rubber-stamped the debasement of meat.

All along government officials took the view that it was not their job to demand that meat manufacturers keep up certain standards. They preferred to allow firms the right to do what they liked, and simply reveal the composition of the product on the label. As a result, standards have hardly improved but the manufacturers no longer need to fear arousing the interest of the trading standards watchdogs. In most cases the truth about adulteration is now on the pack, but in some cases it can all too easily be hidden in the small print of the ingredients list.

It is not only our traditional ham which the government has failed to protect. A host of other meat products are not what they should be, and yet they have been given the moral backing of the law.

Roast beef can be swollen with water before cooking to end up the consistency of a wet flannel on the delicatessen counter. Wet bacon, which shrivels, concertina-like, under the grill, is now a legally protected species. Even raw meat – joints, steaks and mince – may now be pumped with unnecessary water.

The only proviso to all this adulteration is that the manufacturer must own up to his methods or to his use of extra ingredients on the pack. Although it protested noisily as the new regulations were debated, the meat industry has now recognized that it got off lightly.

Imagine the outcry if other manufacturers were discovered to be regularly tipping water into milk, wine or beer. Would we feel the same about a pint of best bitter 'with added water', even if it were clearly labelled, as we do about dilute bacon, ham and beef? How would you fancy Beaujolais nouveau 'with not more than 20 per cent added water'?

It is astonishing that the Ministry of Agriculture has ignored its role as a guardian of food standards in its regulation of the meat industry, yet in other areas, notably those of dairy products, fats and alcohol it lays down strict rules and, by and large, ensures that standards remain high.

The meat industry had a long time to prepare and argue its case. The Food Standards Committee started a review of the meat products legislation in February 1975. The Ministry did not produce proposals for change until July 1981, and then came up with suggestions so biased in favour of the industry that even some meat firms were embarrassed. One idea was that it would be perfectly acceptable to add 5 per cent water to fresh meat joints without any indication on the label! Another astonishing proposal was to legalize a deception whereby unnecessary added water could be called euphemistically 'additional curing solution'.

Furious arguments from the trading standards service and consumer bodies forced the Ministry to think again. It took it another two years to come up with further proposals, which in their final form were a considerable improvement. But defeating the most ludicrous points served to draw the fire of the consumer lobby. While bodies such as the Shropshire Trading Standards department, which specialize in food law, worked night and day to prove their case, their efforts could not persuade the Ministry to change the whole basis of its thinking. They failed to make the bureaucrats see the need to take more responsibility for the upkeep of standards.

As a result, we will soon see all sorts of strangely named meat products in the sausage, beefburger, pâté and meat-pie cabinets which have very little meat. The meat slurry mechanically recovered from waste bones is still being used as if it were lean meat, with no indication of its presence on the pack. Watered ham and bacon is still in the shops, and not all of it has to own up to its true composition. And arguably worst of all, we will still find some of the nastier bits of the carcass used, quite legally, as meat.

What is meat?

Most consumers would be very surprised if they knew what the industry regards as meat. To us, meat is whatever you can buy fresh from the butcher's shop. Muscle is obviously meat, as is liver, kidney, heart and tongue. With some thought we might well add cheek meat, as in a bath chap, and tail meat, as in oxtail, to the list. If we really know our meats we will be aware that pancreas and thymus are glands better known as sweetbreads when derived from lamb. But we would almost certainly raise an eyebrow at the idea of diaphragm, rind, skin, gristle and sinew posing as meat.

Yet all these parts of the carcass are regarded in the new regulations not only as meat, but as *lean* meat. They can be used to make up part of the lean meat content of products as long as they are free of visible fat. So while we may fondly imagine that the lean part of any meat product must be solid flesh, in fact it may be any of the above offals. There is one additional ruling for skin, rind, gristle and sinew, however: they can only be incorporated 'in amounts naturally associated with the flesh used'. But since the manufacturer may choose to use shin, say, which has 19 per cent connective tissue, this is not a very onerous limitation.

The Ministry's definition of meat has even surprised some butchers. It draws no distinction between the glands from a young lamb and those from beef or pork. While some butchers do sell lamb sweetbreads as a speciality, they will throw away the porkbreads and beefbreads as inedible. And a butcher would never sell you diaphragm – it is regarded as only fit for the meat factory. While some butchers do request the offals with their carcasses (just as we might ask for a chicken with its giblets) the diaphragm has never traditionally been included since it is not regarded as saleable.

Meat manufacturers who do use it prefer to call it 'skirt', but it is not the same as skirt steak, which is the muscle between fillet and sirloin. Nor is it 'goose skirt' either, the strip of flesh connecting the two back legs of an animal, which may also, occasionally, be found on sale in mince. The diaphragm is a thick, tough circle of muscle which divides the chest cavity from the abdomen and which, in days gone by, would have been used only for pet food.

You will see no reference to diaphragms, glands or rind in the ingredients list of any meat product. If they have been used they will almost certainly be hiding under the general heading of 'meat'.

If you are surprised by what may be described as lean meat, you will be astonished at what can go into cooked-meat products such as pies, pasties and canned stew. The list includes such unsavoury items as intestine, lungs, rectum, testicles and udder. Manufacturers do not have to own up to any of these specific parts of the carcass. They may simply describe them all under the heading of 'offal' in the ingredients list.

When you realize what manufacturers may use as meat it brings an altogether different meaning to such items as commercially manufactured lamb stew, beef sausage or pork pie. And claims that products are '100 per cent beef' are less reassuring when you remember that this does not necessarily mean the beef flesh you expect, but could be all sorts of distasteful parts of the beef carcass.

Some even more nasty parts of the animal may not be classed as meat, or offal, but there is still nothing to stop them being used in meat products. Waste parts from the head such as ears, eyeballs, snout and lips may all go into our food quite legally . . . but there is just one proviso. They must be labelled as such. And since there is probably no great demand for meatballs with added eyeballs, or pork pie with a pinch of snout, you are not likely to come across them in the ingredients. However, in the past one or two firms have added these stomach-turners *illegally* by not owning up to their presence, and of course there is nothing in the new regulations to prevent unscrupulous firms from breaking the law in this way. What is worrying is that they are usually detected only if they have been added to mince, since the particles are still large enough to be identified under a microscope. Once they have been ground finely and cooked it is almost impossible for our public analysts to spot them. In tests they would appear to be just meat. So a rogue firm might be tempted to include such items in its recipe in order to replace part of the meat content and thus cut costs.

Definition of meat (according to H.M. Ministry of Agriculture)

Mammals

Flesh	Pancreas
Fat	Tail meat
Diaphragm	Thymus
Head meat (muscle meat and	Tongue
associated fatty tissue only)	Skin ⎱ in amounts
Heart	Rind ⎰ naturally
Kidney	Gristle ⎱ associated with
Liver	Sinew ⎰ the flesh used

Birds

Flesh	Neck
Fat	Skin ⎱ in amounts
Gizzard	Gristle ⎰ naturally
Heart	Sinew ⎱ associated with
Liver	the flesh used

N.B. All the above, apart from fat, may count as lean meat as long as it is free from visible fat.

Offal which may be used in cooked meat products

(in addition to those parts of the carcass listed above)

Brains	Rectum
Feet	Spinal cord
Intestine (large)	Spleen
Intestine (small)	Stomach
Lungs	Testicles
Oesophagus	Udder

How can fat be meat?

When the Food Standards Committee finally reported on the

meat products industry in 1980 it was very concerned about the amount of fat that went into some items. Manufacturers would buy container-loads of waste fat from the slaughter-houses and use it to stretch out their sausage, pie and pâté recipes. Fat was no longer being used at any sort of natural level in some products. The meat content of many brands of sausage, for instance, was often more than half fat. Since the committee's report was published, little has changed.

True, we now have a few brands of meat products which claim to use low-fat recipes. But this is no thanks to the government. They have been produced as a voluntary reaction to the growing consumer awareness of the link between diet and health. And they are still very much the minority. Despite the new regulations, the container-loads of fat still find a ready market.

What the committee wanted to change was the legal definition of meat. The problem was that under the old regulations 'meat' was defined as flesh *and* fat, and on analysis even 'lean meat' was allowed to contain up to 10 per cent fat (because of the difficulties of stripping every single shred of fat from a piece of meat and because fat is present within the muscle). Most meat products had compositional standards. For instance, a pork sausage had to be 65 per cent pork, of which half had to be lean. So 32½ per cent was supposed to be lean – though up to 10 per cent of that could be fat – and the other 32½ per cent simply had to be meat, which meant all of it could be fat. So altogether a pork sausage could have been 35.75 per cent fat and only 29.25 per cent lean. Not only that, but any manufacturer could add in extra fat, over and above the meat and lean requirements, to bulk up his recipe.

By changing the legal definition of meat, the Food Standards Committee realized it could put a stop to the unhealthy practice of 'fat pumping', as it was known in the trade. According to the old regulations, meat was 'flesh, including fat, and the skin, rind, gristle and sinew in amounts naturally associated with the flesh used'. While the chewy bits were limited to their natural proportions in the chosen cut of meat, fat was one and the same thing as flesh.

The committee commented: 'We do not think that such loose wording should continue since it permits the addition of fat in excess of the amount allowed to be included in the meat content without any requirement to declare its presence in the list of ingredients. We consider that the definition of meat should limit the fat . . . to the amount naturally associated with the flesh used and that any additional fat should be so specified in the list of ingredients.' So the committee felt that fat should be treated in just the same way as sinew and gristle, and limited to the proportion naturally found in the associated cut of meat.

Did the Minister listen to this recommendation from his specialist committee? Given that it had spent five years considering the question, did he bow to its good judgement? He did not. Just as before, the new regulations allowed fat to be classed as flesh and put no natural limit on its use. That is why the average sausage today tastes just the same as it did a year ago.

The Minister did take note of the committee's other point and agreed that additional fat should be listed as an ingredient where it was used over and above the meat content to add bulk to the remaining ingredients. But a few weeks before the new regulations were due to come into force, a selection of minor amendments slid quietly through the parliamentary machine and changed this provision. At the moment popular meat products which have minimum meat quotas do not have to own up to extra bulking fat.

The net result of all this is that despite all the 'minimum 80 per cent meat' type of labels now so much in evidence, the fat pumping still goes on. 'Meat', it is sad to say, can equal 'fat', and those impressive claims provide no real insight into the quality, or the healthiness, of the product. Again the Ministry missed its chance to legislate to improve standards. It has simply enabled manufacturers to mislead us even further by offering them some impressive wording options without prevailing upon them to improve what is inside the pack.

But all may not be lost. The Ministry may have failed to put a tighter limit on fat in meat products, but at least it may be about to force all manufacturers to tell us how much fat is present. A totally different set of regulations, currently under consideration at the Ministry, proposes that all food products with more than .5 per cent fat should own up to the quantity, and tell us whether the fat is saturated (the type linked with heart disease) or polyunsaturated. If these proposals become law all meat products would have to be labelled, though it is highly unlikely that the statement of fat content will be given nearly as much prominence as the present statements on meat content.

Gristle, skin and sinew

Remember canned steak when nine out of ten pieces were either stringy, fatty or both? And who can forget the delights of the old-fashioned sausage when each mouthful would offer a delectable nugget of hard gristle? Those were the days.

Nowadays meat manufacturers would not dream of palming us off with such nasty ingredients . . . at least, not in any way that we would notice. Instead they have developed all sorts of machinery to turn chewy bits into something that will slip down our throats unnoticed. Some machines boil down chewy bits into a glue-like paste, others grind them up until they resemble fibres of real meat.

Parts of the animal that used to be deemed fit only for pet food are now valuable commodities in the meat-manufacturing business. Slaughterhouses have a ready market for their animal skins and rind (pig skin), as well as the gristly, sinewy off-cuts from tough carcasses. Old dairy cows, ewes and sows often come into this category, and a large proportion of our cheaper meat products will have come from these sources.

Whether this is a welcome development is debatable. If we accept that we have to make the best possible use of the food we have, then it is better that manufacturers find ways to make every scrap of meat edible. The problem is that by doing so, they have extended the possibilities for debasement and fraud.

In the days when gristle and sinew could always be detected by the customer's teeth, their use was self-limiting; too many nasty lumps and we simply would not buy that brand again. Now, remember, the Ministry has said skin, gristle and sinew may be used in place of lean meat, as long as their proportions do not exceed that which would normally be found in the particular cut of meat used. That gives the manufacturer more scope than in the days when just a small amount of gristle would lose him trade. If he chooses to use shin of beef, for example, the allowable proportion of connective tissue is as high as 19 per cent. The chewy bits may not have as much flavour as lean meat, but that is easily taken care of . . . an extra pinch of seasoning, perhaps some artificial flavouring, and the customer will never know.

There is still no guarantee that manufacturers will stick to the permitted proportions of connective tissue. Analytical tests are improving, but they do not always reveal an excess. Trading standards men are especially concerned about the use of rind, which they suspect may often be used over and above the amount 'naturally associated with the flesh'. Where a product is under suspicion, trading standards departments will ask the local public analyst to carry out tests, and the basic test for meat is the nitrogen test. The problem is that because lean meat, connective tissue and rind all contain similar amounts of nitrogen the results of this test will not differentiate between them. They will simply tell the officer whether the meat content is at the correct level. If it is, some departments will delve no further. Their limited finances mean they cannot afford to test products *ad infinitum*. But it is now possible to test specifically for rind and gristle by looking for an amino acid called hydroxyproline. It acts as a marker of their presence and because it can prove very accurate, many departments are now starting to ask for this test to be done as a matter of course.

But perhaps we should not worry about eating gristle and rind. After all, it is just as good for you, isn't it? Sorry, the answer is . . . no. The meat industry is very keen to emphasize the message that meat is a protein-rich food with an impor-

134

tant part to play in a healthy diet. It will tell you enthusiast-ically that we rely on meat for a third of our average daily intake of protein. But it is less than keen to admit that gristle and rind are not nearly so nutritious, and can come up with some very puzzling answers to embarrassing questions.

Ask the manufacturers, and they will tell you that rind, for instance, actually has a higher protein count than lean meat. According to the Meat and Livestock Commission, pork rind is 38.3 per cent protein, while lean beef, lamb and pork are 20–21 per cent protein. It makes you wonder why we don't all feast on rind in preference to roast beef! But those figures are very deceptive.

First, the water content of lean meat is much higher than that in raw rind, and so the protein value is, in a sense, diluted. When meat is cooked it loses water, and so its protein count goes up to about 30 per cent. On the other hand, when rind is cooked it absorbs water, and its protein count comes down to below that of lean meat, and may be as low as 20 per cent. So by the time we eat it, rind is definitely not as high in protein as lean meat.

But there is another point the meat manufacturers do not make clear. Neither rind nor any other connective tissue has the same biological value as lean meat. In other words, the quality of its protein is not the same. Some of the amino acids which make up protein are either missing or very low in connective tissue, notably tryptophan and methionine, which are essential to health.

There is also the question of digestibility. It does not matter how rich in protein a food may be: if we cannot digest it we won't get the goodness. Rind and connective tissue are particularly indigestible, and even when cooked, their digesti-bility is lower than that for lean meat.

Then there is fat. Even when rind is carefully trimmed, it contains nearly twice as much fat as lean meat, yet it can be used as if it were lean meat. Given all we know about the health implications of eating too much fat, this can hardly be classed as a nutritious substitute for lean meat.

None of this stops certain manufacturers from using mountains of chewy bits in their meat products. The processing and distribution of rind has lately become an important industry in its own right. Once pork would be sold by the abattoir with its skin attached, whatever its destination. Now only a few butchers' carcasses retain the rind. The vast bulk of pork is stripped of its skin immediately after slaughter, only to be reunited at the meat-processing plant.

Advertisements regularly appear in the trade press for fresh and powdered rind products. Separate companies have been set up specifically to buy pigs' skins from the abattoirs, process them, and sell them on to meat-product manufacturers. At a 1985 meat trade seminar involving 47 companies from the UK and Eire it was revealed that an astonishing 77 per cent of the manufacturers who attended used rind in their products. It may go into sausages, beefburgers, pies and pasties – and it would not need to be separately labelled.

Apart from its cheapness, rind has one other great advantage for the mean manufacturer – it will soak up water like a sponge. The most common method of incorporating rind is to cook it gently until it has softened and swelled, cool it, and then chop it finely. During the cooking it may absorb its own weight of water, which is trapped as the collagen fibres melt to form a gel. That gel may be flaked or chopped and used in that form, or it may be turned into an emulsion with fat and water.

Until now, manufacturers have simply ground or chopped their rinds, skin, gristle and sinewy pieces as finely as possible before incorporating them. They call the roughly chopped results 'comminuted'. But technology can now give them a texture which is just like that of lean meat.

By flaking the nasty bits into tiny strands they 'can resemble cooked solid muscle meat', according to one of the companies promoting a flake-cutting machine. At a recent trade exhibition this company showed how sinewy meat could be flake-cut and used in hamburgers, steaklets, etc. without the customer ever knowing. Under the heading 'General Advantages' its brochure lists some revealing points.

Raw materials with high percentage of connective tissue can be used with assurance that the end product will be tender and palatable.

Cohesive properties of flake-cut meat are such that no binders are needed, however binders and nutritional extenders can be used when desired for specialized products.

Flake-cut meat has a greater affinity for added moisture than other comminuted meats.

Tenderness and texture of flake-cut meat products can be tailored to meet specifications of bite, texture and appearance.

Flake-cutting maximizes the value of raw materials and upgrades carcass value.

And the brochure's last point is perhaps the most amazing: 'Flake cutting offers the consumer more acceptable products.'

In view of the uses to which just one of the cutting heads can be put, that is debatable. In the technical specifications it is claimed that a three-inch cutter can 'reduce gristle, back strap [a length of yellow gristly fat that runs along the spine], poultry skin and pork rind' to a particular size of flake that will 'produce English sausage, roast beef binder, and meat filling for ravioli.'

Roast beef binder? This refers to the practice of padding out joints of manufactured roast beef with extra cereal, or water, or in the case of this machine a form of meat paste (see below).

Even better than cooked rinds is a rind emulsion, which again can be flake-cut to resemble real meat when it has gelled. Because it includes waste subcutaneous fat or 'flab' fat as well as water, it is even more of a moneyspinner for the manufacturer, and arguably more of a heart-stopper for us (see Chapter 6). An ideal emulsion consists of 5 parts cooked rind, 14 parts mixed pork fat, 14 parts water and one part whey protein. The latter helps to bind everything else together.

Most of us know the difficulties of making an emulsion which will not separate. When we mix together oil and vinegar to make a salad dressing we are making an emulsion, but if we leave it to stand for very long we will usually find the oil has floated to the top and the vinegar has sunk to the bottom. But meat manufacturers have overcome this problem. With the addition of the thick, jelly-like rinds their emulsions are more solid and so more able to trap the water. But the emulsion itself also helps the meat mixture (known as batter) to absorb and hold water. In a series of articles for *Meat Industry* magazine three Dutch technologists explained why rind emulsions can be so useful:

The presence of very finely comminuted and emulsified fat in the fine meat batter can improve considerably the water binding. A possible explanation for this is that the very fine fat globules, when fully integrated within the network of muscle fibres and fragments, . . . significantly reduce the normal shrinkage on heating. This also partly explains the fact that meat batters in which part of the fat has been pre-emulsified with water and milk protein always have better water and fat binding than batters to which these constituents have been added separately.

In other words, because the fibres in the chopped-up meat mixture are coated with fine particles of fat they are less likely to lose water as they cook. And fat added to the meat as an emulsion will work better than fat simply added on its own.

The most common use for a rind emulsion is the sausage, but not everyone will stoop so low. The champion sausage-maker Keith Boxley believes traditional methods produce the best-tasting sausages. 'I'd say the real recipe for success is playing fair with the customer. We always aim for 80 per cent real meat content – no rind emulsions or rubbish. Of course it costs a bit more, but people are used to Marks & Spencer these days and Mrs Jones will pay for quality when she can find it,' he said.

It is important to remember that his attitude is shared by some manufacturers, too. Not all firms are determined to produce the cheapest recipe possible using the nastiest ingredients. No one makes sausages from fillet steak, but some manufacturers do stick to traditional recipes which do not include rind, gristle or unnecessary water in their products. The problem, for them as well as for us, is that we cannot tell.

Because makers do not have to admit to such unappetizing
ingredients, the scrupulous producers must depend on our
taste buds to spot the difference.

The extrusion intrusion

Meat batters may be added to sausages, burgers and other
meat products to help bind ingredients together. But their
main purpose is far more alarming. Technology has enabled
manufacturers to make use of these jelly-like pastes to replace
the real meat content of dozens of everyday products. Science
can deceive the eye, the brain and the knife and fork! Next
time you come across a cube of meat, in a pie, say, which is
dark brown like steak, has the fibrous texture of steak, and
tastes like steak, do not jump to conclusions. There is no
guarantee that it *is* steak.

Extrusion technology can create almost anything from this
meat paste. Veal escalopes, meat balls, barbeque ribs, slabs,
slices and cubes of steak may all be products of this invention,
yet the customer can rarely tell the difference. As we have
seen, the texture is provided by the cutting machines, which
turn tough meat, gristle, fat and rind into fibrous strips. The
use of emulsion techniques helps to trap in water, to give the
produce weight and what the manufacturers call 'juiciness'.
And the use of binding agents (in some products) such as
whey protein (though it could be soya, cereal or another form
of milk protein) enables all the ingredients to be bound
together in a stable mixture.

This mixture is then extruded, like toothpaste, into moulds.
Little square moulds will produce the lumps of 'steak' that
might be in your pie, round moulds the meatballs. Large oval
moulds will produce a 'joint' which can be cooked and sliced
for the type of meat you find in a typical steak sandwich. The
latest moulds to cause a buzz around the industry will
produce strips of 'ribs', without the bones.

Extrusion techniques have also intruded on many of our
canned meat products, they have found their way into frozen
meals, and they may be diced and dehydrated to form the

meat portion of dried curry, risotto and other dried dishes. Many meaty-looking canteen meals are, in fact, these clever concoctions of meat, fat, rind and gristle, all finely ground and shaped to look like hunks of steak, or escalopes of veal, or burgers.

The quantity of lean meat used in the mixture will vary according to the product. In a meat pie, only 50 per cent of the meat content has to be lean by law, and the meat content may be as low as 16 per cent of the pie's weight, if it is uncooked. This means that manufacturers can legally get away with using meat scraps naturally containing gristle, sinew and skin for half their pie-filling mixture, and use more rind plus fat for the other half. Yet to the consumer it seems like real steak when it is covered in gravy and pastry.

Only pies, sausages, burgers, chopped and corned meats, pâtés, luncheon meats and spreads have legal minimum levels of meat (see chart, pages 182–3). Every other meat product can have as much or as little meat as the manufacturer wishes. Surprisingly, meatballs, and the frozen or dried ready-meals, are not covered by any compositional standard at all. The new law demands only that the manufacturer state his chosen meat-content level on the pack, and that at least 65 per cent of that meat content is lean.

Of the more upmarket products, such as steak sandwich slices, ribs and veal escalopes, again there are no compositional standards. But a manufacturer could run into trouble from another law if he drops his meat content too low. It is a basic provision of the Food Act that food should be 'of the nature, quality and substance demanded' by the customer. And the Trade Descriptions Act insists that the name of the food must not mislead the customer. A veal escalope, if it were so labelled, might not be of the 'expected quality' and would surely be misleading if it were only half veal, and the rest an emulsified mixture of pork rind, soya and fat. That would certainly be the view of the trading standards officers. But the rights and wrongs of food descriptions are never clear-cut. As each new product comes along it often takes a court case to establish that a description is misleading. And it is frequently the experience of the watchdogs that some manufacturers prefer to err on the wrong side for the sake of greater profits, and accept the fine if they are caught out.

There is no risk of a prosecution when meat products are sold from a catering establishment – a pub, restaurant or works canteen. Although the new law insists that manufacturers give caterers the same information about what they are buying as they give to customers in shops, the right to know does not have to be passed on to the diner. So there is unlikely to be any change in the current practice of passing low-meat, high-fat products along the cheaper end of the catering trade.

For all these products, as long as the meat manufacturer keeps within the legal limit for the lean-meat content he can use his extrusion machines to his heart's content (though arguably, not to ours). As customers we have no legal right to know whether the cubes of steak in our pie are real pieces of steak or cleverly combined mixtures of steak and other less delectable delicacies. The manufacturer does not have to state the methods he has used, or single out gristle, sinew and rind for mention on his ingredients list.

The industry argues that if it was to tell us exactly what it puts in meat products it would put us off eating them unjustifiably. It regards its role as performing a valuable public service by using up the protein waste from animal carcasses. And it points out that if it were to stop using offal, fat and rind in its recipes we would have to pay far more for our meat products. All this may be true, but is it not up to the customer to make a choice rather than for big business to decide what is good for us?

Blood and bone

The boffins have been hard at work creating protein from other products which would more usually be channelled into the fertilizer and pet-food trade. In the past, blood has only been used in black pudding, in which it is included in liquid form. But recently far more slaughterhouses have been carefully collecting blood for specialist firms who turn it into a powder which can be used in any meat product. There are two types of protein which can be extracted – that from whole blood, and that from blood plasma. Neither have the effect you would expect: if blood protein is added to sausages, for example, they do not turn dark red. In fact, although it is now believed to be used in quite a few pies, sausages and cheaper products, it is virtually undetectable by the customer. The treatment means that the powders give very little colour, flavour or texture to the product, but they do add nicely to the nitrogen content.

The extraction of bone protein is a very new process in which the protein trapped within bones is released from the solid mineral elements around it. The powder can go into meat products, where it will soak up water or fat, and it is even possible to produce meat-like fibres from an emulsified mixture of this bone powder by spinning and chopping it.

Odd though it may seem, there is nothing illegal about the use of either of these substances. Blood and bone are perfectly permissible as ingredients in food as long as they are not used in place of meat. Strangely, the meat regulations have nothing to say on the subject of blood and bone, but since they are not listed amongst those parts of the carcass which *may not* be used, the implication is that they are allowed. However, they are not listed amongst those parts of the carcass which *may* count as meat, either, and so cannot be used to replace any part of the stated meat content. Since they do not count as meat, they ought to be separately listed within the ingredients panel, but again this is not clarified.

Why the Ministry chose to ignore bone and blood is a mystery, and a point of considerable frustration for the enforcement officers. By not making the law crystal clear, they fear the bureaucrats may have encouraged some under-hand practices to gain momentum. Some time ago the Shropshire Trading Standards Department found that state-ments by bone-protein manufacturers revealed a potentially fraudulent attitude to their use in the meat factory. One description suggested that, 'one per cent of (X) bone protein + 3.25 per cent water replaces 4 per cent of lean meat.'

The temptation to cut corners with both products is obvious. Since bone and blood are protein, they will pass the analyst's basic nitrogen test as if they were lean meat. So manufacturers might hope to include them in place of the legal requirement of meat, and get away with it. In fact it would take an analyst with strong powers of intuition to spot a product containing either blood or bone. Both products are available on the open market and trading standards men are convinced they are being used to replace meat by a number of fraudulent firms. But nothing has been proved.

The problem is that there are so many variables when testing meat products which must each be taken into account. After the analyst has checked the nitrogen level he will probably work out the amount of cereal, soya or milk protein that may be present, and adjust his figures accordingly. It is highly unlikely that any of his mathematical calculations will point to the presence of blood and bone, and most analysts say they have to rely on a 'sixth sense' that something is not quite right. If the alarm bells do ring, the tests for bone and blood are so sophisticated, and therefore so expensive, that the trading standards department is more likely to try to prove their existence by an unannounced visit to the factory.

Curds and whey

Another protein booster comes from the waste products discarded by the dairy industry. The whey left after cheese-making, for instance, no longer gets tossed to the pigs when they are alive. Instead, it is tossed into some pork meat during its processing. In fact whey protein may be added to anything from hams, sausages and pies to sliced turkey or chicken roll.

Most of the milk proteins used in manufacturing are extracted from pasteurized cheese whey. They are concentrated, filtered and spray-dried to form a useful, and very inexpensive, powder which has become extremely popular in the ham-making business. It has a dramatic effect on the water-holding properties of all meat – no one quite knows why – and as we have seen in the emulsification process, it has the curious ability to lock particles of fat into the meat mixture.

One well-known dairy company makes no secret of these dubious advantages. In its promotional literature for the trade it lists the 'benefits' of using its product in sausages and cured or cooked meats:

– reduced cooking losses through improved binding;
– natural enhancement of the meat flavours;
– smooth, even texture leading to improved slicing and appearance;
– succulent mouth feel;
– simply declared as Whey Protein Concentrate.

The new law says that if milk protein is used in any whole meat cuts, like ham or roast beef, then it must be mentioned clearly on the front of the pack, and that has deterred some processors. They feel it would put customers off buying their product. Others feel that the extra profits it brings outweigh the disadvantages. According to a trade hand-out from a milk-protein producer, the powder used at a rate of 3.1 per cent in ham will help to bind in 30 per cent water and will cost only 1.7p per lb of product. Given current ham prices, that helps producers and retailers to bring in at least 50p per lb extra in profits. But even higher gains can be made when milk is combined with more bulky fillers to add weight and water to our meat.

'Meat and two veg'

Wheat and soya have given an entirely new meaning to the well-worn phrase 'meat and two veg'. Traditionally, meat products such as sausages have always been a mixture of meat and vegetable protein. In the old days it was usually some sort of cereal which was used to bulk out the sausage. Now soya is creeping in as well, not only into sausages, burgers, pies and canned meat, as you might expect, but into some far less likely products, including hams and joints of cooked roast beef.

Ironically, while more and more of our meat products are

padded out with cereal and soya, pet-food manufacturers are dropping them from their recipes. Our pets do not like to find lumps of 'bakery products' in their meat, and pet-owners, it seems, have taken the hint and are now avoiding brands which contain them. The human palate is obviously not so discerning.

Soya is the success story of the 'eighties. During the 'sixties and 'seventies soya oil became increasingly popular as its importance as a source of polyunsaturated oil became known. But what was to be done with the bean mash left after the oil had been extracted? Two processes were developed. In one, the beans were given a texture just like meat. Called TVP, textured vegetable protein, it is often sold as a nutritious alternative to mince, or burgers (you do not have to be vegetarian to enjoy soybean curd burgers), although there is still a long way to go before they produce a product that will fool anyone's tastebuds into thinking that it is the real thing.

In the other process the soya protein is extracted, usually in powder form, and used in small proportions in combination with meat, in such items as burgers. To the manufacturer it has two special advantages: it will absorb water and fat, and it will not shrink on cooking. If a brand contains added water you will often see that it also has soya. Pork pies often make use of soya's magic properties rather than gelatine nowadays, to soak up the fat which seeps out during cooking. If you have noticed that a certain brand of pie seems to have more pork and less jelly, it is not necessarily because the manufacturer has had a fit of generosity. It is more likely that he has started using soya, which keeps the pie-crust well filled.

Of course, any extra cereal or soya, as well as the added proteins, should be honestly listed in the ingredients, but there will always be companies who 'forget' to mention its presence.

One West Country firm marketed a product it called 'beef steaklettes' and claimed on the pack that these, in line with similar products, were 'all meat'. On first analysis it appeared that the firm was telling the truth. The nitrogen count, which is the basic test for the presence of meat, was up to the mark. But further tests revealed that some form of vegetable protein was present, and that this was masking the true meat content. In fact, the product was only 60 per cent meat, and its maker was successfully prosecuted for describing it dishonestly.

The difficulty of differentiating between meat and non-meat protein is a constant problem for public analysts. The nitrogen test only measures the amount of protein present, and if some of that is suspected to be of vegetable origin, more complicated, and therefore more expensive, tests have to be done. Often a manufacturer who wants to cheat may choose to substitute only a tiny fraction of his meat content with soya or cereal, yet this will be enough to boost his profits handsomely. Shropshire Trading Standards Department, in a report to its County Council, describes the system used by a local firm a few years ago.

In one particular instance a beefburger-type product, which by law should have contained a minimum of 80 per cent meat, was found to be apparently genuine when first submitted for analysis. Further enquiries however were undertaken which revealed a meat deficiency when the quantity of vegetable protein contained therein was determined. The manufacturer was successfully prosecuted . . .

The economic advantages to the manufacturer can be illustrated by reference to this investigation, which revealed that a mere 1 per cent less meat in the product than required by law, saved the manufacturer around 620 lbs of meat per week or the equivalent of one whole cow. The actual deficiency on the sample in question was over 5 per cent.

Nothing in the new regulations will put a stop to this type of fraud, nor could it. No matter how strict the law, there will always be someone who will bend the rules. Those rules still say that if any type of non-meat protein is used it must be specified in the ingredients list, in descending order of weight.

As long as we are told of its existence, there is clearly nothing wrong with eating cereal or soya in products where it would be expected. But it was the unexpected use of non-meat protein which caused a storm of protest when the regulations were under consideration, and is still a sore point amongst those whose job is the upkeep of food standards. Over the last ten years a practice has grown up which is nothing short of blatant adulteration. Whole raw joints of meat may be laced with cereal, or soya, in order to add to their weight. Joints of pork or beef, boned turkeys and hams are put through a dividing and restructuring process which allows the small individual muscles to become saturated not only with water, but occasionally with these cereal 'extras'. The technique, known as 'tumbling and massaging', is discussed more fully in the next section, but suffice to say its main aim is to add as much weight as possible to the meat for the least cost and maximum profit.

What bothered the trading standards service most was that the final appearance of the meat as a ham, slice of cooked shoulder, turkey roll or joint of meat gave no hint of its true composition. Even the description was sometimes designed to mislead the customer. One north of England importing company was fined £300 in 1981 after admitting it had falsely described ham padded out with cereal and extra water as 'old-fashioned cooked ham'. This, the first case to highlight the practice of adding cereal to ham, involved a Belgian manufacturer. But it was not long before other firms followed suit in order to compete on the same price terms.

The answer, as far as the Ministry was concerned, was simply to force the manufacturers to own up to the true contents. So the new regulations insist that 'where any person sells any meat product which has the appearance of a cut, joint, slice, portion or carcass of raw meat, cooked meat or cured meat . . . the name of the food . . . shall include an indication of the ingredients used.' This is why we now see labels on some cooked meats which say 'with added cereal'. It also explains why some are marked as having 'added milk protein', too.

However, the real question is why we should allow the addition of cereal in the first place, if its sole purpose is to aid the debasement of a traditional product. It comes back to the fundamental disagreement between the Ministry and some of those concerned with the quality of our food. Should we throw standards out of the window and accept that anything goes as long as it is accurately and honestly labelled? Or do we draw a clear line below which manufacturers may not sink?

There are very good reasons for sticking to the clear line approach. For a start, even with truthful labelling (and there is no guarantee that it will be), competition could still lead to the demise of some of our best-loved foods. Ham with extra cereal is usually a lot cheaper than the genuine stuff, and few of us can afford to disregard the price completely. While 'padded ham' takes sales away from real ham the price of the real thing will remain unnecessarily high. And it is a sad reflection on all of us, but the fact is that labels are not read all that often. Stacking the trolley in a busy supermarket is not the best time to start worrying about whether a brand of ham says it contains cereals or not, and if it does, whether by buying it we might be contributing to the demise of real ham.

By abandoning standards for ham the Ministry has cleared the way for the debasement of other products. Might we see dairy products go down the same path in the near future? Maybe the Ministry will allow manufacturers to call any concoction 'cream', no matter what is in it, as long as any extras are listed on the label: 'double cream – with added chalk' perhaps? Don't laugh, it could happen.

There was another solution to the controversy over 'padded ham', but the Ministry ignored it. Rather than ban the process altogether, or adopt the approach it did, the government might simply have ruled that any cured leg of pork with added cereal (or water, for that matter) could not call itself by the traditional name 'ham'. Since it is a hybrid product, somewhere between ham and luncheon meat, it surely has no right to the trading advantage of calling itself by an age-old description. The same might go for any traditional name. So 'cooked roast beef' and 'roast pork' could be reserved only for meat which has been roasted in the time-honoured way without unnecessary extras. But new-fangled products, such as turkey and chicken roll, might be allowed the extras as long as they are labelled as at present.

It will be a long time before the Ministry overhauls its meat legislation again. But sufficient public pressure against some of the worst aspects of the new rules could easily bring about some amendments. We can only hope that we do not all become so accustomed to adulterated products in the meantime that we never see the return to real meat.

Steaks, steaklets and steakettes

At the top end of the processed meat market are the fabricated steaks. For these, the flake-cutting technology is used to turn older, tougher beef into tender 'steak'. Often a little extra water is added to give what the trade euphemistically calls 'succulence'; sometimes seasonings are added, and a few even contain cereals or soya, though they now have to own up to that fact.

Those that do not contain padding generally make great play of their 'all meat' status, and imply that they are simply top-quality lean meat which has been tenderized by chopping up and reshaping. Phrases such as 'choice meat', 'pure beef', and 'prime lamb', for example, are much in evidence on the packs, but nowhere do you see any suggestion that the product may contain chopped up gristle, ground-up skin, diaphragm, head meat or oxtail. Bear in mind that *any* of these items may be used in a product which may still legally be labelled '100 per cent beef'.

Of course, some of these products may well be wholly made up of tender lean meat. But it is unlikely. Such meat would not need the chop-and-shape treatment in the first place. Some may be relatively lean pieces of tougher meat. But there is no way to distinguish them from products to which the manufacturer has been tempted to add any old rubbish, safe in the knowledge that the process will provide the perfect disguise.

Many of the product names are very misleading. In a recent trading standards survey, one brand of 'ribs' was only 86 per cent meat, a pack of 'chicken breast steaks' consisted of just 67 per cent meat, and some beef sandwich slices, cheekily labelled 'British beef at its best', were only 65 per cent meat.

It was the breakthrough in inventing flaking machines

which led to this latest group of meat products. When meat was chopped or ground, the best you could get was a solid-pressed burger consistency. But the claims for flake-cut meat machines are surprisingly true. They *do* produce a texture which is very close to real meat.

One machine manufacturer claimed in the headline of an advertisement, 'Now you can create "steak" '. And he went on to say: 'By using this flake-cutting machine, you can flake any boneless meat, poultry, or seafood. You can then re-form the product into steaks, chops, roasts, or any shape you wish . . . Now you can create "steak" from meat trimmings.'

Surely, you may be thinking, it would be illegal to use the word 'steak' or 'chop' to describe a product that is not a cut of fresh meat. Used on its own it probably is. The Food Labelling Regulations state that 'the name of the food shall be sufficiently precise to inform a purchaser of the true nature of the food and to enable the food to be distinguished from products with which it could be confused'.

There is no doubt that a mixture of chopped meat, moulded into a steak-like shape, might be confused with real steak. And the same goes for mashed pork moulded into a chop shape or a rib shape, lamb moulded into a cutlet shape, or poultry moulded into breast or leg shapes. As a result, marketing men have recently dreamed up a plethora of silly names which incorporate the word 'steak' without their actually using it on its own. So you will now find 'chopsteaks', 'chipsteaks', 'snacksteaks' and 'clubsteaks' . . . even 'dallas-teaks' on the shelves. Fake steak is by far the most popular of these fabricated products, but you can also see 'imposters' such as 'lamb grills', 'riblets' or 'pork chop shapes'.

There are no legal guidelines for standardizing descriptions for such products, or for stipulating minimum meat content, and there is no requirement for the manufacturer to own up to the quality of meat he has used. This is an appalling omission, since in 1980 the Food Standards Committee called for strict rules on how these products should be labelled.

In its report on meat products it said: 'We accept that the ability to increase the palatability of tough meat can be regarded as in the public interest, but it could be open to abuse by less scrupulous manufacturers. We take the view that the consumer should be told when re-formed or restructured meat is used. In our view it is important that, because of the treatments they have received, such products should not be confused with fresh meat cuts direct from a carcass. We recommend that the use of meat which has been re-formed or restructured should be declared by means of the inclusion of the term "re-formed meat" in the description of the product.'

This was not the first time that a form of words was suggested. Back in 1975 the Association of Frozen Food Producers had been far-sighted enough to realize the potential confusion in putting chopped and moulded 'steak' next to real steak in the freezer. It had come up with a code of practice for its members which meant that any meat which had been chopped, minced or ground up and then re-shaped to look like a whole piece of meat should be described as 'chopped and shaped'. It allowed the use of the word 'steak' but insisted it should either be put into quotes, or given an asterisk which would tell the customer of its true nature.

While this was a step in the right direction at the time, by 1980 the numbers of 'fake steak' products had dramatically increased, and they could be found alongside fresh meats in the cabinets as well as in the freezer. The Food Standards Committee felt the words 'chopped and shaped' just were not good enough. 'Whilst the Code is generally to be welcomed, we cannot endorse some of the recommendations made,' said the Committee. 'In particular, we think that "chopped and shaped" is not sufficiently meaningful to convey to the consumer that the meat used is re-formed. We also take the view that the use of the word "steak" for such products is misleading even though it is qualified by inverted commas or an asterisk.'

In the absence of any law on the subject, the trading standards service was becoming increasingly concerned about the number of these products coming on the market. It was worried that many customers were under a misapprehension that these dishes were always lean meat. And it disliked the

151

way the word 'steak', which has a very specific meaning, was being used to describe everything from poor-quality beef-burgers to steak-shaped products made of lamb or pork with no beef in them at all.

Many trading standards departments felt it was time to prosecute firms for their misleading descriptions. But where were they to draw the line? Was any manufacturer of a chopped-meat product likely to be in breach of the law if it described it as steak? Or were they to allow manufacturers to use the word as long as what they described did not contain extra ingredients such as cereal or soya? And what if a chopped and shaped product called itself 'steak' when it was not beef but lamb, or pork, or turkey? Since the law gave no written guidance it was up to the watchdogs to decide whether they felt an offence had been committed and then try to prove it to a court of law.

Clearly it would have been counter-productive if one trading standards department had been lenient while another took a strict line. It was time for their co-ordinating body, LACOTS, to agree a common approach. In December 1984 it was decided that when the word 'steak' was used on its own it should refer only to a single, thick slice of beef. When it referred to other types of meat the species should be named, so the label would have to say 'lamb steak' or 'pork steak'. Chopped and moulded products could only use the word 'steak' if it was part of a longer name, like 'quicksteak' or 'jiffysteak', and only then if it were at least 95 per cent meat with no added cereal.

The code laid down by LACOTS still stands and is purely voluntary. Manufacturers know that if they keep to it they will have nothing to fear from the legal watchdogs. But is it good enough?

Apart from frozen meat products there is still no firm directive that meat which has been chopped up and possibly mixed in with skin, gristle and sinew, and then moulded into a natural-looking shape, must make that treatment clear to the customer. In the US the law insists that these products must be clearly labelled 'fabricated' – a word that gives a much better idea of their true nature than the rather vague 'chopped and shaped'. Given that they have been around for at least the last ten years, and that six years ago the government's own committee pointed out the necessity for informative labelling, it is astonishing that the new Meat Product Regulations ignored the problem completely.

Most brands do follow the codes and make a voluntary confession that the product has been 'chopped and shaped' or 'flaked and formed', but the phrase is often hidden in the small print. One recent survey by North Yorkshire Trading Standards Department discovered that the lettering for such announcements is sometimes up to ten times smaller than the lettering of the product name. The same was true if the manufacturer had to make the compulsory statement 'with added cereal'.

Some items which might appear in the chopped and shaped brigade in the future would not even be classed as meat products! If they were 100 per cent meat, no matter how grisly its origins, they would not be covered by the new regulations at all. This is the result of a badly phrased definition of meat products in the explanatory schedule to the regulations. Under the heading 'Foods which are not meat products' it lists 'Raw meat to which no ingredient, or no ingredient other than proteolytic enzymes, has been added'. In other words, if meat has added cereal it counts as a meat product, and must obey the regulations; if it has added water it is a meat product; even if it just has a shake of salt and pepper it is a meat product. But if it has been diced, ground, slurried and then pressed back together again, but nothing other than meat has been added, it is *not* a meat product and may evade the new law. This ludicrous loophole might just appeal to some cleverclogs of a manufacturer who decides he does not want to stick to the provisions for a minimum quota of lean meat. He could, in theory, use even more rind, gristle and sinewy pieces to make his 'steaks', 'ribs' and 'cutlets' than is used at the dubious end of the sausage and burger trade. The Ministry may have opened the door to even more debased products with impressive-sounding names.

9

Water, water, everywhere

Just about anything you eat contains water. Bread is 40 per cent water; chips are 47 per cent water; tomato ketchup is 65 per cent water. None of them would be what they are if manufacturers pumped in vast amounts of extra water in order to increase their weight.

But somehow the same rules do not apply to meat products. Thanks to modern processing, a cooked, cured leg of pork may be anything from 40 per cent water to 80 per cent water, and the two extremes as alike as chalk and cheese, yet both will call themselves 'ham'.

The same is true of the uncooked product. A cured side of pork may gain an extra 30 per cent liquid during the curing process or lose a full 5 per cent from the amount of water present when raw, and yet the results of each method will call themselves 'bacon' despite the fact that under the grill one will shrink to a fraction of its original size while the other will remain virtually the same size as it was in its uncooked state.

An average joint of lean beef is 68 per cent water when raw, and between 40 and 60 per cent water when roasted in the usual way (it all depends whether you foil wrap and cook slowly). But let some processors do the roasting and it will come out with 75 per cent water and be as soggy as a wet flannel. Yet the two types of joint may both be called 'roast beef'.

These three products suffer the most from the added-water scandal, though other processed meats have fallen victim too. While many people believe the new Meat Product Regulations have now sorted out the problems, the truth is, they have only served to set a seal of moral approval on a practice which degrades our meat.

The new law, which came into force on 1 July 1986, sets no legal limit on the amount of water which can be pumped into meat, even though it is almost always a blatant consumer fraud. The law simply makes do with a requirement for manufacturers to mention the extra liquid on the pack or, if sold loose, on a ticket close by. The idea was that if manufacturers had to own up to the unnecessary water they use, they might think twice about using so much.

Certainly, some companies have now lowered the water content of bacon, ham and other cooked meats so that they are not forced to make such an embarrassing declaration to their customers. Others have swallowed hard, put the statement on the pack and continued with their watery methods. In most cases the percentage of added water does not seem too bad to the uninitiated. Few hams and roast meats confess to more than 15 per cent extra water, and most bacon, if it carries a declaration at all, is usually below 10 per cent water.

Yet these seemingly low figures hide one of the most subtle consumer con-tricks ever perpetrated. In a fudge of figures, the government has given *carte blanche* to the meat industry to continue watering down our meat to an appalling degree. But in the way those figures are expressed on the label the debasement has been given an acceptable face.

Ready for the mathematics? Let's start with cooked ham, which is covered by regulation 9 (2) (a) of the new regulations:

Cooked cured meat [shall be marked] with a declaration in the form 'with not more than z per cent added water', there being inserted in place of 'z' such number expressed as a multiple of 5 as makes the declaration an indication of the maximum added water content of the food.

OK, we have already seen the words 'with not more than 5 [or 10] per cent added water' on some hams, so now we know the legal reason behind the phrase. But what exactly is 'added water' . . . added to what? You might think, quite reasonably, that it means any liquid which has been added during the curing process. Wrong! Or you might think, even more reasonably, that it refers to any extra liquid that you would not find in traditionally cured ham. Wrong again!

This is how the new law defines 'added water':

For the purposes of these regulations, water that is present in a meat product, whether the meat product is cooked or uncooked, shall be regarded as added water to the extent, and only to the extent, that the quantity of water present in the product exceeds the quantity of water that would naturally be present in the meat used in the product when raw.

In other words, if the cooked ham has more water than when it started off as a raw leg of pork, then the extra water must be declared. Since a boned leg of pork is 60 per cent water on average, any ham with up to 65 per cent water should be labelled 'with not more than 5 per cent added water'. And if it is above 65 per cent and below 70 per cent then it should be labelled 'with not more than 10 per cent added water' and so on. However, this ruling is not only exceedingly silly, it could mean extinction for what is already an endangered species, genuine traditional ham.

On the face of it, using the water content of raw pork as a benchmark for calculating added water appears to be a good idea. But it presumes that unadulterated ham should have the same water content as the raw meat. And nothing could be further from the truth. Most of us, surely, do not want ham that has the consistency of raw pork, which is far too wet to produce any depth of flavour. As we have seen, a leg of raw pork is about 60 per cent water. Old-fashioned York ham, if you can find it, is just 40 per cent water. Perhaps a better comparison would be with the sort of plain, honest ham you can still get cured and cooked by a butcher or specialist firm. The water content of this delicious type of ham is about 50 per cent.

When you think about it, there is no earthly reason for cooked ham to have as much water as raw meat if it is prepared traditionally. It takes 10 per cent of liquid brine to cure the pork, though much of this should drip out and evaporate as the ham is left to mature. And then the ham must be cooked, which, if it is done properly, will be in a dry roasting oven. Any meat will lose 10–20 percentage points of water while roasting, so it is perfectly natural to expect a good cooked ham to be 50 per cent or less water.

So the Ministry has set its benchmark far too high. Rather than taking the water content of the traditional product as the starting point, it has opted for a water content in the middle range of adulteration as its norm. Of course, the manufacturers would have hated the idea of setting the benchmark at the level of the traditional product, since they would have been forced to confess to added water on almost all their ham. So to appease big business, the Ministry has left at a competitive disadvantage the smaller firms who are still trying to make the traditional product.

While one ham sitting on the delicatessen counter may be 50 per cent water, its next-door neighbour may be 60 per cent – and that makes a big difference to the taste. Yet neither will be obliged to carry any declaration about added water. As far as the customer is concerned, they both appear to be of the same quality, so he or she is likely to choose the one with the lowest price tag, and the chances are that that will be the semi-adulterated product rather than the traditional type.

Other cooked meats, like the roast beef you might buy sliced from the delicatessen counter, also have to own up to added water only when it is in excess of the level found in the raw meat. And in their case the benchmark is even more crazy. After all, meats such as turkey, roast pork or roast beef do not have to be cured. They do not need the injection of any liquid before they are cooked. In a normal roasting process they should lose between 20 and 40 per cent of their water content as the heat and gentle drying process brings out the full flavour of the meat. So you would normally expect them to be somewhere between 40 and 50 per cent water after a genuine roasting. Yet the new regulations allow cooked meat to be about 60 per cent water without having to make a declaration. The manufacturers may have pumped them with ordinary water before cooking, and used new technology to steam-cook them, and yet the Ministry says the rubbery

157

results need no qualification on the label. No wonder butchers who still appreciate the taste of properly roasted meat are up in arms over the Ministry's mathematics.

By the way, if you are trying to follow my arithmetic and you have got lost, I will explain that last bit. (But if you're happy to trust me you can skip this paragraph!) First of all, different joints of beef have different water contents, mainly because their fat content varies, so I have opted for round figures. But if you say a joint of beef has a water content of 60 per cent, and during the roasting process it loses a maximum of 40 per cent, it does not end up, as you might have thought, with 20 per cent water. Bear in mind it loses 40 per cent of that 60 per cent ($40 \times 60 \div 100$), which is 24 percentage points off the total water content. Hence a joint of beef which had 60 per cent water when raw could end up with no less than 36 per cent water when cooked. By the same token, if the joint loses 20 per cent water, it is 20 per cent of 60 per cent, ($20 \times 60 \div 100$), which is 12 percentage points off the raw water content, making 48 per cent water when cooked. And if you are with me so far, you may have realized that I have still over-simplified matters, since the final weight of the meat, after all that dripping and evaporation, must be lighter than the original weight of the raw joint. So the final percentage of water content will be a few points higher. That is why I have rounded up the figures to between 40 and 50 per cent.

Worst of all is the bacon situation. The mathematics are even more complicated here because the industry succeeded in arguing that because the curing solution is not cooked off, it needed a benchmark that was higher than the water level of raw meat. So the Ministry came up with an extra 10 per cent 'tolerance level' before the manufacturers have to admit to added water. It works like this. Let us say the water content of a side of pork is 60 per cent (in fact it varies a lot from the belly to the back according to its fattiness). It will be injected and soaked with curing solution, of which about 4 per cent will be curing salts (sodium chloride and nitrate/nitrite) and the rest will be water, probably between 10 and 15 per cent. If, by the time the pork has matured into bacon, more than 10 per cent extra water remains, then that remainder has to be labelled as added water.

You may think this sounds fair, until you realize that bacon of old was not more watery than raw pork. It tended to have about the same, or slightly less, water in it than the raw meat. How? Again, it comes down to the change in processing methods. When bacon was made in the back kitchen it would have been rubbed manually with the curing salts for weeks on end, and finally hung until mature. Even when it was soaked in a salt solution, it was still traditional to wash off the brine and dry the bacon in a cellar until it was ready to be eaten. Butchers who make their own bacon still use that method, and report that after dripping and drying the water content comes back to the same level you would find in raw pork.

This is borne out by the figures published in the food technologists' invaluable guide, *The Composition of Foods*, produced jointly by the Ministry of Agriculture and the Medical Research Council. The two bodies analysed various foods for water levels, among other items, in the late 'sixties and early 'seventies, before the worst excesses became commonplace and they found that bacon did not normally have more water than raw pork. For example, a dressed carcass of raw pork was 50.7 per cent water, while a dressed carcass of bacon was 48.8 per cent water. Rather than absorbing extra liquid from the cure, the bacon had *lost* slightly more than had been pumped in.

The same is true when you look at water values for individual rashers. Pork belly, for instance, was 48.7 per cent water, while for the equivalent streaky bacon rashers the water content had *dropped* to 41.8 per cent. So by allowing the manufacturers to sneak an extra 10 per cent water into bacon without telling us, the Ministry has put its official rubber stamp on a debased product.

But it does not end there. Even if you allow manufacturers to use a method whereby no liquid is lost from the bacon during curing, they still do not need a full 10 per cent tolerance level. When the regulations were just proposals, the trading standards service argued long and hard that 10 per cent added water was too much. Manufacturers only needed to use 10 per cent *salt solution* to effect the cure, and since that would be made up of 2–5 per cent salts and only 5–8 per cent water, an allowance of a full 10 per cent extra water was over the top. In effect, manufacturers were being allowed to make their curing solution much more watery than it need be, while still not having to own up to added water. The Food Standards Committee, in its 1980 report, was adamant that a 10 per cent curing solution was enough to do the job.

'The equivalent of 2 per cent to 3 per cent by weight of dry curing salts is needed to cure ham.' it said, 'although exceptionally, some hams contain as much as 5 per cent of curing salts. If the salts are added in solution, a total allowance for the curing solution of not more than 10 per cent in the final product would be appropriate to correspond to the quality of traditional ham.'

Its obvious concern for quality and traditional standards was not echoed by the Ministry in its regulations. Despite all the expert argument, it stuck to the notion that 10 per cent water, not salt solution, was needed to cure bacon, and in so doing gave the trade yet another legal device for adding unnecessary, but highly profitable, water to meat.

It does not end there, either. Let us say, for the sake of argument, that a manufacturer uses 5 grams of salts and 10 grams of water to cure 100 grams of pork – in other words, a 15-per-cent curing solution – and it is all absorbed. You might think that is the absolute top limit he can get away with before he has to declare added water. But it is not. You need to ponder on a bit more arithmetic to understand why, I'm afraid.

Regulation 13(1)(c) of the new law states: 'the added water content of a meat product is the total weight of added water in the product expressed as a percentage of the total weight of the product as sold.'

Note the words 'as sold'. If 10 grams of water and 5 grams of salts have been pumped into the meat, then it will be that much heavier when it is sold. So 100 grams of pork would become 115 grams. And since the added water has to be expressed as a percentage of that final, heavier weight, it will not be 10 per cent but 10 divided by 115 . . . which works out at 8.7 per cent added water – well within the no-declaration-necessary limit.

All this means that a manufacturer can add 16 grams of curing solution to each 100 grams of pork, made up of 11 grams of water and 5 grams of salts, and still be comfortably within the 10 per cent limit for added water. And according to the trading standards experts, that is 6 grams more water than they actually need.

How they persuade meat to absorb all that water, and hang on to it, sometimes right through the cooking process, is all due to the amazing technological breakthroughs of the last twenty years. And that is what we come to next.

The injection technique

The meat industry has come a long way since the first strip of needles injected curing solution into a side of pork. Nowadays injection machines have a bank of up to 800 needles which can inject a fine spray of solution throughout the meat at high pressure. And they claim 'dosage rates' of up to 80 per cent, almost doubling the weight of the meat. A piece of pork, thus injected, can be seen to swell unnaturally under the flood of water from these giant pincushions.

One reason why the meat can absorb so much liquid is the aerosol form of the spray. The needles penetrate right through the flesh, and as they are slowly withdrawn they spray a fine mist of solution around the cells.

One injector, which claims to be 'the ultimate machine available', offers:

– 138 needles in 6 rows;
– automatic depth control of needles for hams with skin;
– injection rate: from 5 to 80 per cent.

Other manufacturers say, 'considerable weight gain is thus made possible', and point out that 'the financial advantage is obvious'.

There is little difficulty in getting the liquid inside the meat, then. Making it stay there is a different matter. All the injection needles can do is to swamp the area around the cells with liquid, but they are not fine enough to penetrate the insides of the meat cells themselves. Without help, the water would simply drip out, but with the use of chemicals or massaging techniques, and often both methods together, the cells can be prompted to become bloated with the excess liquid.

Polyphosphates

The real secret of turning water into meat involves the use of these salts. Oddly, no one quite knows why they work, but no one disputes that they do work . . . and how! Rather than the scientists suggesting a new method to the manufacturer, with polyphosphates the usual system has been turned round.

Meat manufacturers started experimenting with these salts about thirty years ago and found they worked particularly well in products such as sausages. They seemed to improve the emulsification process, allowing the fat and water to blend with the meat mixture more smoothly. Soon they discovered that whenever they added polyphosphates they could 'hide' more water in the mixture. Ever since then, the scientists have been trying to figure out how the process works.

They now know that these slightly acid salts are working their magic inside the microscopic meat fibres, known as myofibrils – about a thousand of them make up one of those little meat fibres which we can see with the naked eye. It is the myofibrils which hold the natural water content of the meat, and which can be persuaded to swell and hold on to extra, unnatural water. The swelling is triggered by a certain level of polyphosphate, so that all the water lapping around the outside of these miniature fibres is sucked in and held in the space inside.

Any salts will trigger this process to some extent, but by far the best results occur with a combination of ordinary salt and polyphosphate, which confirms for scientists what many manufacturers already knew – the right combination can prompt the myofibrils to swell to more than double their original size.

The same research has uncovered another mechanism which can have the opposite effect on the myofibrils. In an ironic but pleasing twist, any upsetting treatment handed out to a pig before slaughter can prompt the myofibrils in the pork to contract and so squeeze out some of the natural water. Pigs are more susceptible to stress at the slaughterhouse than any other animal, and the resulting pork is called 'pale, soft and exudative' or PSE for short. It is regarded as a big problem in the processing industry, not least because any subsequent treatment with polyphosphates can never fully reverse the situation. You could call it the pig's revenge!

Many manufacturers add polyphosphates to the curing solution for bacon and ham, introducing them at the initial injection stage and often during the tumbling and massaging, too. But even meats which do not need curing, like beef, pork or turkey destined for the delicatessen counter, will often get a soaking with water and polyphosphates in order to increase their weight before cooking. Some of the raw 'meat-roast'-style products will be given the phosphate treatment, too.

These chemicals have nothing to do with an effective cure. We had bacon and ham long before anyone ever discovered polyphosphates. Whenever you see them mentioned on the ingredients list you can be pretty sure they have only been used in order to water down the meat. And for some meats which, as we have seen, do not have to own up to added water but have nevertheless been adulterated, the presence of these salts is usually the only giveaway sign. If you are not a scrupulous checker of ingredients lists, you may not have noticed polyphosphates in your meat products. But you might well have observed a strange white gunge which seeps out of bacon when cooking. That is often caused by these salts which have weakened the cells. The white stuff is thought to be a mixture of protein and salts which escapes when it is subjected to high temperatures.

Polyphosphates have another invaluable function for the

processor, too. Earlier on in the processing, their effect on protein comes in useful. The scientific reaction is still not fully understood, but even without cooking these salts can encourage a sticky protein called myosin to seep out of the cells and form a glue-like gunge round the pieces of meat. And manufacturers find this phenomenon particularly useful at the next stage of the process.

Tumbling and massaging

Many hams, cooked meat, gammon and some of those raw 'meat roast'-type joints will take a tumble before they are ready for the customer. After injection with curing salts and polyphosphate solution, or just the latter in the case of uncured cooked meats, the small individual muscles will be divided up and put into something approaching a cement-mixer. Inside they will be given yet another dose of curing solution and/or polyphosphate solution and then they will either be tumbled round, like the contents of a washing machine, or massaged by a paddle, like the dough-mixer on a food processor. The process can take anything from 20 minutes to 12 hours, depending on the meat and the greed of the manufacturer.

All this may sound rather strange, but the effects are well worthwhile for the manufacturer. For a start, the pummelling helps to distribute all that loose water around every cell wall, so that the polyphosphates can work their magic more thoroughly. And while they are encouraging the myosin to seep out of the cells, the massaging process brings it to the surface of each muscle as a sticky coating.

And that is not all. Not content with the high percentage of water retention already achieved, some processors are turning to vacuum massagers which can persuade the meat to take in even more unnecessary liquid. Because the meat cells are in a vacuum they expand in order to try to fill the space, and so take in some valuable extra drops.

When the massage is over the processor is left with a pile of sticky pieces of meat, all well bloated with water. All he needs to do is to put them into a mould and the natural protein will glue everything back together again in whatever shape he chooses – the traditional tapering leg-of-pork shape for the ham pieces, a round roast shape for the raw meat pieces, or a large oval shape, perhaps, for those meat pieces which are going to be cooked.

It is at the tumbling stage that extra cereal or milk protein may be added, to help soak up more water; fat and rind emulsions may be poured in, too, at this point. As the pieces glue themselves together again these extra fillers are bound in between the individual muscles in such a way that most of us would never know they were there.

Many manufacturers of cured meats do own up to these methods now, not because the law specifically forces them to do so, but because their trade association has agreed a code of conduct with the trading standards co-ordinating body, LACOTS. Since January 1986 members of the Bacon and Meat Manufacturers' Association have been labelling their tumbled and massaged products as 'ham – formed from cuts of legs' or 'ham – made up from cuts of legs'. And if they have added any extra meat in the form of fine mince or emulsion they must call their ham 're-formed'.

But not every manufacturer follows this code, and those that do are not giving the uninformed customer very much useful information. 'Re-formed' hardly describes accurately the unappetizing treatment a ham may have had, and says nothing about the slurry of rind or fat which may be contained within the meat. Only cured meats are covered, anyway. The raw meat roasts, and various uncured, cooked meats have so far not been urged to make any confessions about their origins. Only a shopper of the calibre of Sherlock Holmes will spot the tell-tale clues.

Roast meat

According to the Meat Research Institute in Bristol, roasting can cause meat to lose up to 40 per cent water. It is enough to bring tears to the eyes of a manufacturer who has gone to such lengths to make his meat absorb extra liquid. The whole point of injection, tumbling and massaging is to get water inside the meat fibres and keep it there until we buy the product. If he is simply going to cook off all the water by putting his precious commodity into a hot, dry oven he might as well not bother.

Needless to say, many manufacturers have developed ways of roasting their beef or pork which do not actually involve roasting. Instead they steam the meat to keep in as much water as they can. But just to give the outside a roast-like appearance they will pop the meat into an extremely hot oven for just a few minutes. It is called flash roasting, and while many feel it gives them the legal justification for calling the meat 'roast pork' or 'roast beef', they will have lost no more than 7 per cent of their profitable liquid.

At a trade exhibition, a representative of one of the companies manufacturing flash roasters told me, revealingly, 'There's very little moisture loss with one of these ovens. You're not using it to cook the meat. All you're trying to do with one of these is kid the public on that the meat's been roasted.'

That is the kind of deception to which the government has given the green light by allowing roast meat to have the same water content as raw meat. And if you think that is bad, some so-called 'roast meat' has never seen the inside of an oven at all. It has simply been steamed and that dark brown, well-cooked colour has been painted on with food dye. At least this little trick did not get the government's seal of approval in the new regulations. Trading standards officers can prosecute firms for a false description if they have the cheek to call their painted meat 'roast'. But because it is difficult to catch the cheats, the practice is still widespread at the less reputable end of the trade.

Water in poultry

Of all meats, only frozen chicken is legally prohibited from containing excess water. Thanks to an EEC directive, it may not have more than 7.4 per cent extra water hidden in the frozen carcass. But, idiotically, fresh chicken is not covered by the same rule. And other poultry, such as turkey, duck and goose, whether frozen or not, can contain as much water as it likes. The only legal proviso is that it mentions water in the ingredients list, though it does not have to say how much. Unlike other meat, poultry does not even have to own up to added water on the front of the pack, so there is nothing to stop the producers doubling the weight of any turkeys, ducks, geese and fresh chicken with what comes free from the tap as long as they label it.

Frozen chicken was singled out for punishment after numerous producers realized they had found the key to untold riches! The freezing process was an ideal way to hide that 'miracle meat', otherwise known as H_2O, inside the bird. Customers only discovered they had been cheated when they got home and defrosted the chicken, and even then it was not always obvious that up to 40 per cent of the bird's weight may have dripped away down the sink.

For many years, the worst offenders argued that they could not prevent the uptake of water during the freezing process. After slaughtering and removing the entrails, the carcasses would be quickly chilled in a plunge-bath of cold water, and immediately the dripping birds would go through the freezer before being packed. It was hardly surprising that great lumps of ice were often found inside the cavity – ice which the customer would have paid for at chicken prices.

The protests of consumer campaigners slowly brought about a change. A new method was developed, called dry-chilling, which, as its name suggests, did away with the need for the plunge-bath. The birds tend to be more expensive, but pound for pound they often give more chicken for your money.

In response to the new law, those companies using the water-chill method have had to find ways to ensure enough water drips off before the bird goes into the freezer, to meet the legal water limit. The penalties for cheating are massive. In December 1985, a London importing firm was fined £1000 and had to pay costs of £589 because it brought in a batch of

French chickens which had an average of 40 g more water than allowed.

To their credit, British chicken producers with only one exception have so far kept within the law on added water. After so much bad publicity, they decided to polish up their image by launching 'Quality British Chicken', which is guaranteed free of polyphosphates and is scrupulously checked to ensure a minimal water pick-up. About 80 per cent of the chickens in the shops have the QBC symbol, which is often the only way we can tell a British bird from its foreign rivals.

But trading standards watchdogs are keeping a careful eye on imports from France, Germany and Denmark, where many producers are known to be flouting the law. Unless they are caught, British chickens lose out on the supermarket shelf. An average 2½-lb well-watered continental chicken costing £1.50 may be a worse bargain than an unwatered British version of the same size costing £2. The trouble is that if imported birds are in breach of the law, the customer has no way of knowing. And the simple device of just avoiding foreign birds is not always so easy. Many foreign chickens have British-sounding brand names, and often have the importer's address on the back of the pack.

British chicken producers are so bothered about the situation that they have formed their own watchdog group to scour the country for illicit foreign birds. But while they are keeping their halos well polished, some producers of turkeys, ducks and occasionally geese are still allowing their birds to gather large amounts of water in the dunking process. All we can do is watch out for that giveaway reference to water in the ingredients list and try to do some hasty mathematical comparisons with dry-chilled birds, on the assumption that the water-frozen fowl will be roughly 10 per cent more water and less meat than the dry-chilled variety. It is not easy, and you can be sure the Ministry bureaucrats who decided not to bother including turkeys and other fowl in the new law have never been faced with an O-level arithmetical teaser in a busy supermarket with a toddler or two in tow.

Soggy or succulent?

At the height of the added-water debate meat producers insisted they were doing the customer a favour by watering down their meat. People preferred their ham 'juicy' and their cooked meat 'succulent', they said. But they never came up with any published proof that this was the case.

On the other hand, numerous consumer-protection departments around Britain did surveys and taste tests which proved the opposite. One of the best was by South Yorkshire's watchdogs in 1983. They asked teams of testers from the region to give their verdicts on a variety of different hams and cooked shoulder slices. The most watery of the samples were rated 'wet', 'slimy', 'artificial-looking', 'of poor appearance' and having a 'chewy texture'. Funnily enough, the words 'juicy' and 'succulent' did not merit a mention at all.

The succulence argument did not wash with the Food Standards Committee, either, when it reviewed the problem of water in food in 1978. Its report said, 'Manufacturers claim that these processes enable them to produce products which are less fat but which because of retention of the added water are moister and therefore more acceptable to popular taste than they would be without the use of polyphosphates. We do not believe that all consumers agree with this view and complaints are frequently made that some modern ham has a rubbery texture and lacks flavour.'

Even so, the new rules have not stopped a lot of producers from continuing to use euphemisms like these to describe meat products which have been watered down. Wherever you see these descriptions it is worth checking the pack for that tell-tale phrase 'with added water' or the ingredients panel for a mention of water. Remember, the higher up the list it comes, the more weighty the addition.

It is only by checking the information given on the label, and a good deal of reading between the lines, that the customer can hazard a guess at the true nature of the meat he or she is buying. Added cereal, soya or milk protein in what appears to be a whole piece of meat is a good indication that it has been tumbled. Polyphosphates in the ingredients list, especially if they are in a middle-to-high position in the list, are often a clear sign that the manufacturer is trying to water down his meat, even if it does not come into a category which has to declare the existence of added water. And if you notice that flavour enhancers have been used in something that should be as naturally tasty as bacon, ham or cooked beef, you can be pretty sure the product is awash with extra water.

10

MRM: poisonous timebomb?

The glue industry has a lot to answer for. In days gone by, glue manufacturers would pay meat processors for their leftover bones, cart them away and boil them up. It was a time-consuming and very smelly operation which often caused vehement protests from people unlucky enough to live within a two-mile radius. So the glue-makers developed new methods. Nowadays most glue is made from the by-products of the petroleum industry.

And where have all the bones gone? Why, they have gone to help fill up our sausages and pies, of course.

We have already seen how the protein can be extracted from the solid part of the bone to make a powder which is high in nitrogen. But on the basis of 'waste not, want not', all the little scraps of meat flesh, sinew and cartilage clinging to the bone can now be retrieved, too. It is called 'mechanically recovered meat' in trade jargon – hence, MRM – and you eat it more times than you would ever imagine.

If you are fond of chicken and turkey burgers, sausages, meat pies, pasties, luncheon meat, pâté, sausage rolls, steaklets, meatballs, ravioli, faggots, salami . . . then the chances are that you have eaten lots of it!

The manufacture of MRM is now an industry in its own right. Specialist firms buy up bones and put them through huge pummelling machines which extract anything and everything that is edible. The bones come from processing plants, often in the slaughterhouse, where the meat is stripped and divided into the basic 'primal cuts'. These generally go to supermarkets, where the in-store butchery departments rarely do their own boning, but simply slice up these large cuts into their own requirements. The meat product industry also takes some of these basic cuts, along with the tougher bits of meat muscle, and much of the offal. The bones will be trimmed by the processor, too, generally by a skilled operator using a small powered knife, and these scraps will form an important part of the lean-meat content of many products. Only then are the bones ready for the MRM makers.

Left attached are just slivers of meat muscle and connective tissue – the bits that even the special stripping knife could not reach – plus the marrow in some bones, and it is this combination which is so desirable to the meat industry. It can be used to form part of the lean-meat content of manufactured products, and no one is obliged to admit to its existence. When challenged, manufacturers point out that they are using up valuable nutritious scraps that would otherwise be wasted. Astonishingly, there are up to 2 kilograms of scrapings on a pig's carcass, and up to 8 kilos on a beef carcass, even after the bones have been carefully hand-trimmed.

Three basic methods are used to recover the bits. The most popular machine in Britain uses hydraulic pressure to make the meat flow away from the bones. It is called the 'press system' and it relies on a huge ram which forces the bones through a filtering chamber under great pressure. Only the soft tissue can escape the squeeze, and this emerges at the other end as a smooth slurry, though the makers like to call it a 'purée'.

Another system crushes the bones into small pieces first, and then presses the mash along a screw, rather like a traditional mincing machine. Again, pressure parts the meat material from the bits of bone as it is forced through a screen. Rather than a slurry, the meat looks more like a mince paste, and because the pressure is not so great there is a little less gristle and sinew in the final product.

The third method spins the bones in a centrifugal force which provides the pressure to separate meat from bone. Like the first method, what comes out is a slurry of meat which has lost a lot of its natural texture.

It is this lack of texture which is one of the biggest criticisms of MRM. Because the machines use such force, the cell walls of the meat rupture and the result is to meat what toothpaste is to mint imperials. Even the second method, which is gaining in popularity, has this effect, though to a lesser extent. Because the meat is in this liquid medium it is the perfect breeding ground for bacteria.

The area in and around bones is known to contain a higher-than-average count of the bugs which are naturally present in all meat. Poultry is especially likely to carry the dangerous salmonella bacteria. (It is one of the reasons why we are always being exhorted to cook poultry thoroughly and not to eat it if it is still pink near the joint.) So MRM is likely to start off with a higher bacteria level than other forms of meat. All the processes cause such friction that they cannot help but warm the meat as it is being recovered, and that may encourage the bugs to multiply. If bones go in at a temperature of 15 degrees centigrade the slurry can emerge at 25 degrees or higher. The presence of marrow, which is a biologically highly unstable substance, also adds to the concern over the food-poisoning risks of MRM.

When MRM was first being made it was the big red-meat carcasses which were used. Scraps of meat from beef and lamb bones were more valuable than anything else and they were added in tiny proportions to sausages and meat pies. Now poultry processors are one of the biggest users of MRM: they can get away with large proportions of chicken and turkey slurry in their products if they so wish. This development raises serious health questions, which the government has failed to tackle.

Another worry is the high level of calcium which has been found in some samples of MRM, caused by the powdered bone which inevitably finds its way into the slurry. This is probably good news for most of us. A little extra calcium in our diet will do no harm and could do some people, whose intake may be deficient, a bit of good. But for a small percentage of the population who are hyper-absorbers of calcium, this extra dose could pose problems. These people have to follow strict diets in order to limit their intake of calcium, and since MRM does not have to be labelled, they could take in unknown quantities when eating meat products.

On the plus side, MRM can be relatively low in fat. Unless it has been deliberately adulterated with fatty extras, it is usually between 25 and 30 per cent fat. Given a choice between padding out our sausages with extra fat and using MRM, it is a fair bet that our arteries are likely to stay in better shape with the latter.

This presumes that certain standards will be kept during the manufacture of MRM. As long as only trimmed bones are used, and the machine pressure is not too high, the fat content should not be more than 30 per cent, and has been measured at as low as 9 per cent. But if manufacturers are greedy they can squeeze the bones to the maximum and end up with a slurry which has a higher proportion of marrow and connective tissue. This could put the fat level up to 50 per cent. There is also evidence that some samples have been as high as 60 per cent fat, and that can only be caused by the maker throwing waste lumps of fat in with the bones. At present there are no legal guidelines on the manufacture of MRM to control either its content or hygiene standards.

Manufacturers are very guarded about their use of MRM, and most prefer to keep quiet about using it at all. They know that the public does not like the idea of this sludge going into their meat, therefore those who *do* use it would rather keep us in the dark. When the matter was discussed by the Federation of Meat Traders in 1983 the Parliamentary Committee was in favour of labelling MRM but the Pork and Bacon section of the Federation, who are the main users, did not agree. They felt MRM should simply be regarded as meat, and not separately identified.

The British Meat Manufacturers Association takes the same view. It claims that the question of MRM is 'under constant review', but as it is meat the Association sees no reason to label it separately, or to limit the amount which may be used.

When the government was considering its proposals for the meat product regulations that industry view won the day. Despite the fact that MRM has become widely used in the last five years, and there is enormous consumer concern about eating it, the Ministry chose to ignore its existence when drawing up the regulations. There are no limitations on its use, no rules governing whether it may count as lean meat, or even as meat, no restriction to prevent its use in uncooked products, not a word on how it should be labelled; in short, it just is not mentioned at all. This gigantic oversight flies in the face of the consumer view of the substance, and takes no account of some experts' justified concern over its health risks.

Adding to the confusion are the Food Labelling Regulations which came into force in September 1984. They lay down a number of legal guidelines, some of which could be construed as relating to MRM. For instance, one of the main regulations says: 'The name used for the food should be sufficiently precise to inform a purchaser of the true nature of the food.' Arguably the name 'turkey sausage' for example, might not be sufficiently precise if, in fact, the contents were wholly MRM. And another regulation states: 'Where a purchaser could be misled by the omission of an indication . . . that a food has been dried, freeze-dried, frozen, concentrated or smoked, or has been subjected to any other treatment . . . the name of the food shall include or be accompanied by such an indication.' Again it might be possible to argue that mechanical recovery counts as an 'other treatment' and ought to be indicated.

Probably the strongest reference to MRM comes at another point in the regulations which says, 'Where a purchaser could be misled by the omission from the name used for an ingredient of any indication which, if the ingredient were itself being sold as a food, would be required to be included in or to accompany the name of the food, the name used for the ingredient in a list of ingredients shall include or be accompanied by that indication.' What that gobbledegook means is that an item should be given the same name or description in the ingredients panel as it would be if it were to be sold on its own in a butcher's shop. If butchers sold MRM they could not simply call it 'meat', or 'beef', they would have to explain its treatment in order to tell their customers what it was. So it may be argued, according to this part of the regulations, that manufacturers should do the same.

So far, few manufacturers have even considered including MRM in their ingredients panel. Yet the Ministry feels that these vague references put a legal obligation on them to own up if they use it. Just after Christmas 1985 it sent a 'formal view' to the BMMA explaining that the regulations meant manufacturers should now label MRM as a separate ingredient. But the BMMA took no notice. It says (with some justification) that the waffly wording of the regulations is 'open to interpretation' and it would rather wait and see what the courts decide.

It will be up to the trading standards officers to put the regulations to the test by taking a case against any company which uses MRM but fails to list it. And the watchdogs are mildly hopeful that they might succeed, but it will be a complicated, time-consuming and expensive prosecution. The government could have made their job a lot easier by having the courage of its convictions and spelling out its attitude to MRM. If it had tackled the problem, instead of sweeping it under the carpet, both consumers and the trade would know where they stood.

When the Food Standards Committee made its report on meat products to the Ministry in 1980 it was clearly worried about the likely results of not curbing the use of MRM. 'All types of mechanical recovery destroy, to a greater or lesser degree, the essential structure inherent in hand-trimmed meat so that MRM differs in both texture and behaviour from hand-boned meat,' it said. 'The product may include some bone marrow, and especially if the bones have been ground before recovery, it may have a higher calcium content than other meat, derived from fine bone particles.

'MRM, however separated, is chemically less stable than carcass meat and presents a greater microbiological risk. It cannot simply be regarded as equivalent to carcass meat.'

It recommended that if MRM made up more than 5 per cent of the lean-meat content of a product it should be separately labelled, so that we would know exactly what we are eating. But when the Ministry drew up the regulations, that recommendation fell on deaf ears.

In stark contrast to the British government's couldn't-careless attitude, the United States has adopted firm measures to deal with the problem of MSM (they call it mechanically separated meat). Some products, such as fabricated steaks and corned beef, may not contain it at all, but others are restricted to using no more than 20 per cent MSM to make up the meat content. Not only that, but the size of any bone particles in the slurry is regulated, the amount of calcium must be declared, the fat content is limited, and, most important of all, any product containing it must mention MSM in the ingredients list.

British manufacturers argue that this approach is over the top. They say that there is no risk of food poisoning because MRM is quickly cooled to a safe temperature after its recovery; bone fragments are rare because with most of the machines in use in Britain the bones are not crushed; and in any case the amount of MRM which can be used in any product is self-limiting. The mushy texture and high colour mean that more than 20 per cent of the slurry would affect the eating quality of the final product.

This last argument did not convince the Food Standards Committee back in 1980. It said: 'We have noted that the texture of MRM can be improved by the addition of soya protein products or blood plasma and that the colour can be reduced to some extent in cooked products and we are not convinced concerning the automatic limitations on the extent of use.'

Six years later there is even less reason to be convinced that MRM can only be used in small quantities. Technology has given manufacturers the power to turn soft mixtures back into chewy, meat-like fibres. And the boffins in the food chemical laboratories can now work wonders with their colourings and flavourings. In any case, the high colour applies only to red-meat carcasses. The slurry from pork and poultry carcasses is pale pink and therefore easily disguised in many of the new manufactured chicken and turkey inventions.

Some years ago trading standards officers detected one processed chicken product, being sold to caterers, in which the meat was 100 per cent MRM. They are convinced that this was not a fluke, and that by now there must be others with a high proportion of MRM. Unfortunately, the amount used in a product cannot be proved analytically, but if MRM were controlled by law, it would be up to trading standards officers to make factory inspections in order to catch the cheats.

The real question in the MRM debate boils down to whether we have the right to know what we are buying. While we may accept that MRM is perfectly edible, and reasonably nutritious, some of us may prefer not to eat it. Many of us choose not to eat tripe, or kidneys, or sweetbreads for the same reason. Manufacturers may argue that using MRM is the only way they have of keeping everyday meat products inexpensive. If that is the case, then clear labelling will give us the opportunity of choosing between cheaper brands with MRM or more expensive ones without it. It is clearly not in the consumer's interest to leave manufacturers with the power to decide what is good for us and to make that decision behind closed doors.

11

Changes on the shelf

The new meat product regulations did not simply fail to improve standards. In some cases they have positively encouraged standards to plummet. All sorts of items which are well regulated under the old law have been cast adrift with no legal guidelines on their composition at all. Cans of stewed meat, pie filling, meat loaf, rissoles, meat balls, canned ham and canned mince – to name some of the popular products – may now contain as little meat as their manufacturers care to put in them. Previously, the law stipulated minimum meat contents for all these products and many more.

The new law says only that the manufacturer should label his product with the percentage of meat it contains, but that piece of information will be fairly meaningless to most of us. How many supermarket shoppers know that steak pie filling which is 50 per cent meat is a generous helping, while stewed steak in gravy with 60 per cent meat is on the mean side? And will many of us jump at the offer of meatballs with 45 per cent meat while wisely turning our noses up at canned mince with 80 per cent meat?

What the regulations have done is to ensure that customers are not going to be able to stop the tide of inferior products which are now starting to take the place of their meatier predecessors. Few of us knew what the previous standards were, so we cannot possibly tell whether the meat content in our favourite brand has fallen. The government argued that the new free-for-all approach would mean customers could compare what rival brands had to offer and choose the best bargain. But the fact is, most of us just do not have the time to weigh up all the pros and cons of price *versus* meat content when we do the weekly shop. And as with price fixing, we could get 'meat fixing'. If all manufacturers of a particular product drop the meat content, the fact that some of us may have the patience to compare brands will achieve nothing.

Our trading watchdogs are worried that we could find that some old favourites deteriorate beyond recognition. Sausages, links and chipolatas still have set legal standards. But frankfurters and salami, which used to be at least 75 per cent meat, could drop to below 50 per cent and be padded out with extra fat, cereal and water. The same is true for anything that looks like a sausage but does not use the name. In other words, if a manufacturer makes what to all intents and purposes is a pork sausage, but calls it a 'banger', or a 'porkie', or, if he is feeling very imaginative, a 'breakfast stick', then he can evade the meat standard completely. All he needs to worry about is that his product is correctly described – so that he does not fall foul of the Trade Descriptions Act – and that it is 'of the nature, substance and quality demanded by the customer' – so he is toeing the line of the Food Act. And given those two provisos there is nothing to stop him making a sausage that is under a third meat, and nothing to stop the supermarket plonking it right next to a real pork sausage in the meat cabinet.

Then there are those favourites of the cold-meat counter, chicken roll, turkey roll and the like. In the past we could always count on them to be more than 65 per cent meat, but now some brands are set to drop to 50 per cent meat with the remainder being made up of extra cereal and emulsified fat. They could contain even less meat if the manufacturer feels brave. He has only to label the meat content, and to be able to prove to a court that it is 'of the nature' expected by the customer.

Quality is set to take a tumble on the canned meat shelf, too. Stewed steak in gravy used to have to be 75 per cent meat, and since all these percentages are by weight, it meant that we were protected from buying a product which had a tiny amount of meat swimming around in a lot of gravy. But the standards of this and similar products have been abandoned and the gravy level is rising.

One curious example of how the new approach works involves a foil-packed meat-in-gravy product. Under the old regulations it had to have 60 per cent meat in order to qualify for the name 'sliced meat in gravy'. But because its meat content was not high enough the manufacturers had always called it 'gravy with sliced meat'. That odd description was obvious enough to warn consumers that there was not a lot of solid meat in the pack. But under the new regulations the same product with the same meat content was able to change its name to the much more acceptable 'sliced meat in gravy'.

It is not surprising, then, that although manufacturers fought the new regulations tooth and nail when they were under consideration, they have now realized that in many respects they are better off. The industry view was summed up nicely by the Meat Traders Federation consultant, Anthony Painter, in an article for its magazine. He said: 'It is a fair assumption that most meat traders will regard the Meat Products Regulations with apprehension; something to be endured; another unwelcome legislative burden to be borne; and a further bureaucratic intervention into their trade . . . But it is not all bad news.

'The new regulations will, in a few years' time, be seen as a liberalising measure for the meat trade.'

Just how liberal you can judge for yourself from the charts on pages 182–9. They show how few products still have regulated meat contents. And for those who want to know how far meat standards have fallen by comparing products on the shelf, there is a list of the old meat requirements. Finally, to show how some of the techniques discussed in the last few chapters work in practice, there are some sample manufacturing recipes of our favourite meat products. They are all the type of recipes that would be used for the mass market, though, of course, each manufacturer jealously guards his own formula. And they take no account of the first-class methods that you might be lucky enough to find employed in a local butcher's shop, or by a specialist maker. But even so they show the enormous differences which can exist between well-known brands.

Meat products still regulated by the new law

Product name	Minimum meat/ of which minimum lean	Remarks
Beefburger Porkburger, etc.	80%/65%	80% of burger must be the named type of meat
Economy burger Economy beefburger, etc.	60%/65%	60% of burger must be the named type of meat
Chopped X e.g. chopped ham	90%/65%	–
Corned X e.g. corned beef	120%*/96%	must be all meat
Luncheon meat	80%/65%	–
Meat pie Meat pudding Melton Mowbray pie Game pie	21%/50% (uncooked) 25%/50% (cooked)	smaller pies under 7 oz have lower % of meat
Meat and vegetable pie Pasty/pastie Bridie Sausage roll	10.5%/50% (uncooked) 12.5%/50% (cooked)	–

Scottish pie	17%/50% (uncooked)	–
Scotch pie	20%/50% (cooked)	
Meat paste	70%/65%	–
Meat spread	70%/65%	type of meat must be named and must make up 70% of the spread
Pâté	70%/50%	more fat may go into pâté than into spread or paste
Pork sausage Pork link Pork chipolata Pork sausage meat	65%/50%	80% of meat content, i.e. 52% of sausage, must be pork
Pork and (another meat) sausage/link/chipolata sausage meat	50%/50%	can be a mix of more than 2 meats but pork must weigh more than any other
Beef sausage/link chipolata/sausage meat	50%/50%	half minimum meat content (i.e. 25% of sausage) must be beef
Turkey, chicken, venison sausage/link/ chipolata/sausage meat	50%/50%	80% of meat content (i.e. 52% of sausage) must be the named meat

N.B. 120% is a percentage of the raw meat weight.

Old Regulations for products which now have no set standards

	Previous meat content	of which lean meat
Sausages by another name ('porkies', 'bangers', etc.)	65% (pork) 50% (beef)	50% 50%
Burgers by another name ('burglette', 'meatburg', etc.)	80%	60%
Meat paste by another name ('mousse', 'terrine', etc.)	70%	60%
Canned meat (no gravy), e.g. canned mince	95%	60%
Canned meat in gravy	75%	60%
Pie filling	35%	60%
Sliced meat in gravy	60%	60%
Meat loaf, chicken roll, etc.	65%	60%
Meatballs, faggots, rissoles	35%	60%
Meat in jelly	80%	60%
Brawn, pressed ham, etc.	60%	60%
Canned cured meat, e.g. canned ham	90%	60%

Typical recipes used for popular branded meat products

PORK SAUSAGES

The law says: 65 per cent must be meat, of which 50 per cent must be lean, but since 10 per cent of the lean is allowed to be fat, the required proportions of meat in the total sausage are 29.5 per cent lean (including gristle and sinew): 35.75 per cent fat (including gristle, sinew and more lean meat if desired).

To make a cheap, but legal, variety, take:

28% ....pork back fat and/or flare fat
25% ....pork head meat including gristle and sinew (25% fat)
20% ....water
11% ....rusk
10% ....turkey MRM
4% ....emulsified rind
1% ....salt
1% ....milk protein
.5% ....flavouring (MSG), colouring (Red 2G)
.4% ....polyphosphates
.1% ....preservative

Cook the rinds. Flake or grind into an emulsion using part of the flare fat and milk protein. Put on one side. Add part of the water to re-hydrate the rusk. Chop together the remaining fat, head meat, polyphosphates and remaining water. Add the salt, seasoning, preservative, flavouring and colouring. Mix well. Add the re-hydrated rusk and finally the MRM. Extrude into skins.

The sausage may be labelled 'not less than 65% per cent meat', allowing a 2 per cent safety margin. Pork will head the ingredients list, not fat, since the rind content may be included under this heading and does not have to be separately identified.

To make a quality pork sausage, take:

40% ....pork shoulder meat (20% fat)
29% ....pork back fat

10.5%........rusk
19% ....water
1.4%..........salt, red pepper, herbs and spices
.1% ....preservative

Mix as before. State 'not less than 65 per cent meat' allowing a generous safety margin. May also be labelled 'no artificial colouring or flavouring'.

BEEF SAUSAGES

The law says: 50% of the sausage must be meat, and 50 per cent of that meat must be lean. But again, 10 per cent of the lean is permitted to be fat, and a further proportion may be skin, gristle and sinew. So the real requirements are: 22.5 per cent lean: 27.5 per cent fat.

To make a cheap, but legal, beef sausage, take:

28% ....water
20% ....fat, made up of pork back fat and beef fat trim
18% ....beef head meat including gristle and sinew (75% lean)
17% ....rusk
8% ....turkey MRM
4% ....emulsified rind
2% ....soya
1% ....milk protein
1% ....salt, pepper
.5% ....flavouring (MSG), colouring (Red 2G)
.4% ....polyphosphates
.1% ....preservative

Make as for pork sausage, adding soya to the mixture at the start to soak up extra water. 'Beef' may still be mentioned first' in the ingredients since more than 10 per cent of the water will have been added in the form of emulsified rind and re-hydrated rusk, and the two types of fat can be separately declared.

To make a quality beef sausage, take:

29% ....beef forequarter (10% fat)

27% ....water
25% ....beef fat trim
17.5%........rusk
1.4%..........salt, red pepper, herbs and spices
.1% ....preservative

May be labelled 'not less than 50 per cent meat' (or higher, depending upon the desired safety margin), and may also claim 'no artificial flavouring or colouring'.

BEEFBURGERS

The law says: 80 per cent of the burger must be meat, and 65 per cent of that must be lean. 'Economy burgers' need be only 60 per cent meat, of which 65 per cent must be lean. But remember 10 per cent of the lean may be fat, so the real requirements are, for a beefburger, 47 per cent lean; 33 per cent fat, and for an economy burger, 35.1 per cent lean; 24.9 per cent fat.

To make a cheap, but legal economy beefburger, take:

25% ....shin of beef, including gristle and sinew (15% fat)
18% ....water
15% ....rusk
14% ....beef fat trim
14% ....beef mince, including heart, diaphragm, etc. (40% fat)
9% ....beef MRM (30% fat)
2% ....soya
1.5%..........salt, spices,
1% ....flavourings (including MSG), colouring (Red 2G)
.4% ....polyphosphates
.1% ....preservative

The shin may be flake-cut or finely ground to disguise the 19 per cent sinew it contains. Mix it together with the beef mince, seasonings, flavourings and polyphosphates. Pre-soak the rusk with most of the water and add to the mixture with the soya to soak up the remaining water. Chop the fat separately and blend into the mixture. Lastly, add the MRM, being careful not to overmix.

Product may be labelled 'not less than 60 per cent meat' and 'lean beef' may appear first in the ingredients list.

To make a quality beefburger, take:

56% ....beef forequarter (13% fat)
26% ....beef suet fat
11% ....water
3% ....rusk
2% ....onion extract
1.5%..........salt, spices
.4% ....flavouring (natural beef extract), colouring (beet-root red)
.1% ....preservative

The lean beef may be coarsely chopped to give a good meaty texture, and the top-quality suet (from around the kidneys) will make the product lighter and more flavoursome. The contents are comfortably over the 80 per cent meat level and the use of natural flavour and colour means the product can capitalize on shoppers' current concern about additives and health.

PORK PIES

The law says: a large cooked pie must be at least 25 per cent meat, and half of that must be lean. Smaller pies, and uncooked pies, have various lower percentage standards for meat content.

To make a cheap, but legal, pork pie, over 200 g, take:

55% ....shortcrust pastry
11% ....pork head meat, including gristle and sinew (30% fat)
9% ....pork flare fat
5% ....pork MRM (40% fat)
7% ....water
4.5%..........rusk
3% ....bacon trimmings (30% fat)
2.5%..........soya
1% ....gelatine

1% ....curing salts, salt, seasoning
.6% ....flavouring (MSG), colouring (Red 2G)
.4% ....polyphosphates

Mince the meat and add the chopped bacon, fat, polyphosphates, curing salts, and flavourings. Mix thoroughly. Add the pre-soaked rusk, soya and MRM, and leave to stand for an hour for the curing salts to work. Add the gelatine, fill the pastry case and cook.

The use of polyphosphates in the meat mixture will help to trap the water, and in conjunction with the soya, which will bind in the fat, the meat contents will not shrink, and so the customer will be given an impression of quality. However, this means that the traditional 'jelly' will be sparse, though some gelatine should still be added to keep up appearances. Flavour enhancer is almost certainly necessary in this recipe to offset the tastelessness of the head meat and fat. Colour, too, is needed since the small amount of fatty bacon trimmings is not great enough to give the correct shade of pink.

To make a quality pork pie, over 200 g, take:

46% ....shortcrust pastry
22% ....pork shoulder (25% fat)
15% ....pork belly (75% fat)
5% ....liquid stock
4% ....gelatine
3.5%..........rusk
3% ....cured pork shoulder
1.5%..........curing salts, salt, seasoning

In this mixture the traditional jelly will still appear as the fat seeps into the gelatine, but the better-grade lean meat will give more texture and flavour, making the use of extra chemicals unnecessary. May be labelled 'not less than 38 per cent meat', allowing a 2 per cent safety margin.

12

Tricks of the light, and other good wheezes

The meat machine does not grind to a halt at the manufacturer's back door. While meat product makers have been beavering away to make unappetizing recipes appear delicious, butchers and supermarkets have also developed a variety of dodges to make what they have to offer look like what we want to buy. Some of them might be described as harmless 'enhancement', others are outright fraud.

In the former category is the lighting trick which can turn old, brown meat into what looks like fresh juicy joints. Both butchers' shops and supermarket meat counters often make use of these special fluorescent strip lights, but most of us would never know. They look just like any other strip light and produce rays which appear to be just the same as those from any other bulb. But they can brighten tones of red in an almost magical way. The peachy-beige of a piece of pork turns into a warm rose colour. And the dark purple-brown of beef is transformed into a succulent blood red. But the real magic of these lights is that they do not alter any other colours. The white marble slab is still bright white, perhaps more so, and the sprigs of green plastic 'parsley' remain just as verdant, which would not be the case if the retailer were simply using a red bulb.

The only sign that the shop is enhancing the colour of its meat will be the colour of your hands; under the magic rays your palms will turn a macabre shade of puce, but most of us would be too busy selecting our meat to notice the effect.

There are many varieties of meat lights available, and they are used in two basic ways. The strongest lights are placed directly over the meat counter to produce a dramatic depth of colour. Others are used around the shop or store, where they give the warm tones of natural sunlight to everything on display. Just like real sunlight, they make colours look brighter so that everything looks more appealing. Apples look fresher next to oranges which look juicier and tomatoes which look rosier. There is nothing that does not benefit, but because of a bias to the red end of the spectrum, the colour of meat, delicatessen products, tomatoes, radishes and the like gains the most.

One Yorkshire butcher who uses the sunshine bulbs says, 'they bring out the true colour of the meat, but that's not all. They make everything else look brighter too. Our overalls look whiter, and I'd swear we all look more handsome!'

Scientists developed the lights by experimenting with chemical coatings which were sprayed on the inside of the glass tube, or strip-light bulb. The coating filters the rays, choosing only those which will give the right glow to whatever they illuminate. It has taken five years for the strips to become popular, but now every company selling them reports excellent sales. Every week, more and more are fitted as shops find they boost profits.

Almost all our major supermarkets use a mixture of the two types. Their whole store will be lit with the 'sunlight'-type strips, and their meat counters – fresh, frozen and cold meats – will receive the added boost of the stronger lights. Most of the national butchers' chains, too, use warm lighting for the shop, and strong meat lights over the display. Only in the local butcher's are you likely to view your meat as it really is. Only half our small shops have the strong strip lights over their meat display, and very few use special warm lighting for the whole shop. The expense involved is the main reason for their restraint. Because an 8-foot fluorescent tube costs just over £30, most small shops will either go without, or will invest in only one to go over the window slab.

However, once they have taken the plunge, the users find their money has been well spent. In one survey, the meat department of a large store was lit with two different types of strip light. On one side was an ordinary version that you might find in a domestic kitchen; on the other hung a special strip which simulates sunlight. There was no difference between the two displays, yet a staggering 87 per cent of customers bought meat which had been under the special light. Small wonder one of the bulb firms lists as an advantage of its products: 'The cash register. It will tinkle more often.'

Why should this be so? One reason is psychological. We all know we tend to feel happier and more relaxed when we are in the sunshine. The subconscious part of our brain recognizes that golden light even if we do not, and puts us in the same sort of carefree mood as we fill our trolley. Result? We buy more than we mean to, and from the meat counter we will tend to choose larger joints, bigger packs, and more of them.

The second reason is that we like our meat as fresh as possible, and we (quite mistakenly) link the bright red colour of meat with freshness. In fact, it is only an indication of how recently the joint was cut, not of its age. Before meat is cut the cells are purple, but after a few minutes' exposure to air they turn bright red – the colour we expect. They remain so for only a couple of hours, and then start to darken back to their original purple-brown colour. There is nothing wrong with meat which is a darker red, unless it has been waiting around so long it has started to dry up. But the stores do not mind that they are pandering to our mistaken inclinations. Their only worry is the profit-and-loss account.

Even more ironic is the fact that good meat should not be fresh at all, and that the better its quality, the more likely it is to be the more unattractive shade of dark red. Beef, for example, needs hanging for at least 12 days to become tender, lamb takes five days and pork three. And the longer it has been hung, the quicker freshly cut meat will turn back to its original purple colour.

Yet nowadays it is difficult to find a piece of beef that does not look bright red, especially in the supermarkets. Not only do the stores use special lights, some pack meat in gas in order to prolong its bright red stage. When you buy a joint of meat in a vacuum pack, or a steak, say, on a cling-film covered tray, you can bet that its colour is being enhanced by gas as well as by clever lighting. Nitrogen, carbon dioxide, oxygen and carbon monoxide are the favourites. But while the first three are relatively natural, being found in air and on the surface of meat normally, carbon monoxide is distinctly unnatural. In contact with the juices of freshly cut meat, it forms a bright red chemical called carboxymyoglobin on the surface which will last for days. It has been condemned by two government committees, the Food Additives and Contaminants Committee and the Food Standards Committee, as being misleading to customers. So far, however, no action has been taken to stop its use.

The customer has no way of knowing when gas has been used in a pack – short of sniffing as the meat is opened, and that is not advised! The use of both gas and of biased lighting are successful ways of making us buy meat which, without these techniques, we might otherwise pass over. They are accepted trade practices used widely by the big butchery chains and the supermarkets which, it is strange to say, have never been questioned legally. Yet when the little high street butcher adds sulphur dioxide to his mince to make it appear fresher, he can be prosecuted for his misdemeanour. It is a tough world.

Another little 'enhancement' technique to be found in almost all the big stores is the use of quilted padding paper beneath steaks and chops. It is there ostensibly to mop up any juices which may seep from the meat. But it has the rather desirable side-effect of making the cut of meat look more generous. Although we can all check the weight of the meat we buy, many of us make a judgement simply on appearances. A wedge of thick quilted paper, carefully placed right under the eye muscle of a chop, or under the fleshy part of a steak, makes it look like good value for money.

There is a fine line between what shops regard as good marketing practice and what we might call fraud. The law says food retailers should not mislead us as to the 'nature, substance or quality' of what we buy – either by their written description or by their presentation. Yet supermarkets are rarely challenged. Only one national company has been taken to task for its use of meat padding. In 1984 a chain store was prosecuted after a customer complained about the depth of tissue paper beneath pork chops. It had the effect of making skimpy chops look like thick hunks of meat. The magistrates took a dim view, and fined the store £150.

The change-the-name game

A far more serious fraud happens every day in thousands of food stores and butchers' shops. Most of us have been caught out, often regularly, and misled into paying way over the odds for inferior meat. The trick is to provide cheaper, and therefore tougher, cuts when quality cuts are requested. The innocent customer is however charged the higher price.

It happens far more often than you would ever imagine. A 1983 survey showed that in 80 per cent of cases the customer does not get the type of meat he or she asks for. That survey, which was carried out by Avon County Trading Standards Department, included minor indiscretions as well as major breaches of law. But a survey the next year by Gwent trading standards officers showed that out of 168 shops and supermarkets, one in five was guilty of misdescribing its meat, and 21 instances were so serious that the perpetrators were reported for prosecution.

The commonest cons were passing off lamb middle neck chops as best-end chops, and best-end chops as the even meatier loin chops. In beef the tougher and fattier thick flank area was described as topside, and cheap stewing steak was labelled rump steak. In every case the customer would have lost money, or ended up with a tougher joint – usually both. Strangely, pork rarely suffers at the hands of the change-the-name tricksters, though one notable fraud (see page 197) involved passing off a cut of pork as beef!

The expert investigator for the Avon survey was an ex-butcher, Leslie Williams, who describes himself as a poacher-turned-gamekeeper. He said after the investigation: 'The survey showed that in 19 supermarkets, 21 prosecutable infringements were discovered; in 15 national butchers, 17 prosecutable infringements were discovered, and in 32 private butchers, 77 prosecutable infringements were discovered. As somebody whose livelihood depends on the buying and selling of meat . . . I cannot accept the professional who jeopardizes the standing of his trade by taking advantage of the ignorance of his customers.'

If we all knew as much as our grandmothers knew about how a beast is butchered, these tricks would not be so widespread. But the majority of us could not tell the difference between rumps and skirts, or breasts and necks, when they are on the butcher's slab, or packed on polystyrene. And whenever a customer does not know enough about what she is buying, there will always be unscrupulous tradesmen prepared to take advantage. It happens in the used car trade; it happens in the antiques business; and sadly, it happens in the meat trade.

The Meat and Livestock Commission proved how ignorant we all are when they asked 500 women shoppers to identify eight popular cuts of beef. More than a quarter could not recognize a single one! Only 23 per cent could pick out sirloin steak, and altogether only 50 shoppers managed an all-correct score. Most confused were the under-35s, who tend to buy their meat pre-packed from supermarkets rather than from the local butcher's. And that is the nub of the problem. So many of us are used to choosing our meat from the supermarket cabinet, where it is all made easy for us. We can ponder on the description, pick up the pack and compare the contents as much as we like. In our mothers' and grandmothers' day, customers had to know the cuts of meat in order to know what to ask for. And since times were hard they would buy a larger proportion of tougher cuts (nowadays these go into meat products) and that meant they needed to know how to cook them successfully. In other words, the older generation could have passed an O-level in basic butchery while most of today's meat buyers are still struggling to learn the alphabet.

Our grandmothers were far too canny to pay loin-chop prices for neck chops – and any butcher trying that sort of trick would soon have gone out of business. Not so now. Even when supermarkets have been found guilty of misdescribing meat, it may have taken years before anyone noticed. A local butcher is more likely to have knowledgeable customers (another MLC survey), but they will not necessarily challenge him if he is up to no good. For a start, those of us who know about meat are likely to ask for particular cuts and joints in a way that will make it obvious that we know what we are talking about. The butcher would be foolish if he then tried to palm us off with a cheaper alternative. And anyway, how many of us are so confident about being able to recognize the different cuts that we would be willing to tell an expert that he had made a mistake?

The unscrupulous end of the meat trade has undoubtedly capitalized on our ignorance, and will continue to do so. Although no surveys have been done since 1984, butchers and supermarkets continue to be prosecuted with monotonous regularity for wrongly naming their meats. The following is a selection of court cases from the last 18 months. It represents only a fraction of the trading standards investigations into the change-the-name games.

- In November 1984 a high-class supermarket pleaded guilty to selling thick flank (an inferior roasting joint) under the description 'topside.'

- In May 1985 a small food store in Stockport was fined for selling thick rib (a frying or stewing steak) which had been labelled as 'rump steak'.

- In September 1985 a national chain of butchers was found guilty of labelling silverside as 'topside'.

- In October 1985 a Nottingham butcher was successfully prosecuted for describing fore-rib of beef (from the tougher and fattier front end of the beast) as 'porterhouse steak'.

- In November 1985 a well-known butchers' chain was fined on two counts for selling neck chops described as loin, and for selling thick flank as topside.

- In April 1986 a Portsmouth butcher pleaded guilty to passing off pre-packed best end of neck lamb chops as loin chops. He had hidden the bony best-end chops beneath a loin chop and was fined £200.

The most extraordinary prosecution happened in January 1985, when a small chain of butchers in Birmingham was investigated after a series of complaints from customers. They had bought various cuts of beef, ranging from sirloin steak to stewing beef, all at prices well below the norm. But the beef did not taste quite right, and some suspected that they might have been sold horsemeat. But unlike horsemeat, the steak was slightly lighter in colour than normal beef, and was often described by the seller as 'young beef'. It turned out to be boar pork – from an old male pig whose sexual services were no longer required. Boar pork is a lot darker than normal pork, and if it is very old often has a distinctive and unpleasant taste. It is usually sold to manufacturers at much lower prices than the usual pork carcasses. Yet the chain's customers had been buying this meat for months before the complaints started. The firm and its directors were fined £6000 in all for their deception.

The Meat Trader's Federation gets very heated when tackled on the subject of the meat fiddlers. Understandably, it does not like the idea of its members being accused of skulduggery. It is worried that the misdemeanours of a few will give its many honest members a bad reputation. So it is at pains to suggest why 'mistakes' appear to be made so often. After a damning report in the *Daily Mail* in 1983, under the headline 'Is your butcher cheating you?' the trade fought back, claiming that the sharp practices had been 'blown up out of all proportion'. In a public statement it said: 'The Federation believes that traders who break the law and deliberately mislead the public should be prosecuted.' But it went on to point out that misunderstandings were also possible. 'The meat industry is craft-based and strongly influenced by local traditions. Many cuts of meat have no standard names or definitions across the country.'

This is perfectly true, though it is perhaps not always quite the innocent cause of 'mistakes' that the Federation would have us believe. The fact that meat has so many different descriptions in various parts of Britain is one of the reasons why some butchers feel that they can be flexible when naming cuts. If thick rib has a dozen different regional descriptions (which it has), why not add an extra one to the list and call it sirloin?

The upgrading of meat descriptions cannot always be explained away as genuine regional differences. If they were, you would reasonably expect as many naming errors to be in the customer's favour as against. But in the 1983 trading standards survey every single misdescription was to the detriment of the customer. And in the 1984 survey there was just one instance, out of 37, of a customer being *under*charged when a butcher confused loin with chump chops.

The regional names have been carefully collated by the Meat and Livestock Commission, but their detailed lists serve to show that the dubious practice of upgrading a cheaper cut simply by renaming it is nothing new. Down the decades butchers have clearly been stretching the meaning of the names of better cuts to fit inferior cuts, and they have passed the practice from father to son. For example, what most of us call 'silverside' the East Anglians often call by the slightly more desirable name 'topside'. And while the rest of Britain calls the worst bit of neck of lamb 'scrag', a few butchers in the South East have got into the more profitable habit of calling it 'middle-neck'. North-western butchers are not above using euphemisms, either. They prefer to call the clod (the fatty, tough underside of the neck) by the more edible-sounding 'thick brisket'. Many other regional differences are obviously just local dodges, which, with the passage of time, have now become traditional.

Those of us who do not know much about the cuts of meat often feel far safer in the supermarket. But it may be a false sense of security. The trend nowadays is for supermarkets not to employ trained butchers at all. Previously, all meat arrived in the store in carcass form. But now more and more slaughterhouses have developed processing plants where meat is jointed and often boned before being sold. And some top stores have their own meat depots to cut up the carcasses. Either way, more often than not meat arrives at the back door of the supermarket in what are called 'primal cuts' – the section of loin chops, the boned leg, the pork belly flap, etc.

Relatively little experience of butchery is needed to cut these lumps of meat into joints, steaks and chops, and so the store can employ semi-skilled staff in their behind-the-scenes meat departments. And herein lies the problem. The store's meat staff are in charge of labelling, but with little specialist knowledge their ability to differentiate between two similar joints, or steaks, is bound to be poor.

There is also the problem of deliberate fraud. Just because a supermarket chain appears to be a huge conglomerate, it does not mean that it can never fall prey to the greed of the little man. This can happen in the meat department for a variety of reasons. Most likely it is the need of the meat manager to balance his books. Most stores expect the gross profit from sales of meat to be about 30 per cent, and they will detail exactly how the manager is supposed to achieve this. Each primal cut must produce a certain proportion of saleable meat, with about 5 per cent allowed for unavoidable wastage.

With prices set by head office, his bosses can forecast accurately how much money should go through the cash till from sales of meat. Woe betide any meat manager whose turnover is inexplicably low. The remedy, for the unscrupulous, is to change the name and raise the price. A few dozen best-end-neck chops sold as loin, or frying steak sold as rump, would probably not be noticed under most supermarket systems. And it will cover up for that joint taken home on Saturday night, or the steaks nicked for the barbecue, or it may simply be to hide an appalling mistake in the order, or in the cutting room, which no one dare confess.

This type of fraud does not often happen in supermarkets. The cause of a wrong description is far more likely to be a genuine error, but it is worth remembering that it can happen, next time you think the label on a piece of steak must be gospel.

Upgrading the description of a cut of meat can be very lucrative. There are only so many chops on the backbone of an English lamb. A third are meaty loin chops, a third are best end of neck, and a third are the thin and bony middle-neck chops. Prices in the shops will range from about £2.60 a lb for loin chops, £2.30 a lb for best end, down to about £1 a lb for middle neck chops. A butcher has only to upgrade his chops by one category to make up to £1.30 a lb extra profit. And many customers would be none the wiser.

With beef, the difference in price between thick flank and topside can easily be 50p a lb. The former, generally sold as a pot-roasting joint or frying steak, costs about £1.50 a lb, while topside fetches £2 a lb and more. Rolled and tied like topside, with a layer of codfat (the fat from around the genitals), it is a simple way to make a bit extra cash.

And the other popular con, selling fatty fore-rib steaks as if they were sirloin steaks, is even more of a money-spinner. Fore-rib (the cut of beef that looks like a giant pork chop) is most usually sold as a roasting or braising joint, when it costs less than £1.50 a lb. But pass it off as sirloin/porterhouse steaks and it can fetch £3.40 a lb and upwards. That is nearly £2 a lb sheer profit.

The only misdescription not to earn extra money is passing off silverside as topside. Strangely, these two joints generally cost the same in the shops, despite the fact that there is a marked difference in eating quality between the two. But the wholesale price still reflects the difference, with silverside generally 10p a lb cheaper than topside. Again, it comes back to our ignorance of meat cuts. Silverside is slightly tougher and contains a little more connective tissue than topside, but because it looks identical to the untrained eye, few of us would know one from the other. And because we do not differentiate between the two joints, the butcher has no reason to charge less for the slightly tougher joint.

Short of asking a local butcher to give a demonstration of his craft, it is not easy to become a meat expert overnight. But it is worth getting to grips with some of the commonest cons if you do not want to get caught by the tricksters. You do not have to be able to recognize every single cut. Just learn a few and you will be able to use your little bit of knowledge to spot the rogues. If you can tell the difference between best-end neck chops and loin chops, for instance, and you see the former described as the latter, you have good reason to mistrust the descriptions on other cuts. And you will know to avoid that butcher or supermarket. Here is a guide to the most frequently faked cuts. Study this and you will know how to foil the fiddlers.

The shrewd shopper's guide to the meat cons

LAMB CHOPS

The most popular lamb chops are simply cuts of meat from either side of the back which include a vertebra from the backbone, and often a rib. The scraggiest chops come from the neck end, the leanest from the tail end. The spine is divided into three main sections, middle neck, best end of neck and loin, from which the chops get their names. But because the animal does not suddenly change its conformation just to suit the butcher, there is a grey area between each section, and an overlap of one chop allowed. A few unscrupulous butchers and supermarkets will however allow a whole section to 'overlap' into the more expensive section. The only other types of lamb chops you are likely to find are chump chops and shoulder chops. Although they are quite distinctive, it is not unknown for a greedy butcher to substitute shoulder for chump if he thinks the customer will not know the difference.

Middle neck chops are the cheapest of the popular chops, and so are often victims of the change-the-name routine. They have little meat and a lot of bone, and are so skimpy they should be easy to recognize. Look for the tiny eye muscle which tends to be more round than oval, unlike the others, and the long, flatly-angled rib bone. The small round of muscle will be surrounded by little patches of meat, but there is no streakiness. Since no one is likely to pass any other cut off as neck chops, there are no imposters to watch for.

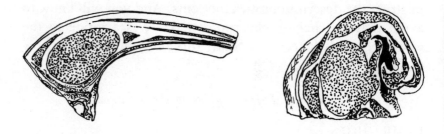

Best end of neck is really the middle of the back. Again, all these chops have rib bones, but just to make things difficult, they may be removed by the butcher! So concentrate on the shape and streakiness of the flesh. The eye muscle should be large and oval this time, and should be surrounded by streaks of meat which extend up the length of the chop, just like streaky bacon.

Likely imposter: middle neck chops

Giveaway signs: ● eye muscle too small
                 ● no streakiness

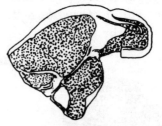

Loin should be easy to recognize by its lack of rib bone – but be careful. 12 out of the 14 chops have no rib bone, but the two nearest the best end do have rib bones. You would be wiser to look at the shape of the main red muscle. There

202

should be one large oval eye muscle, and a smaller one next to it, making a generous triangular shape. The base of the triangle should be bone, and the only streaky meat should be on the tail end.

Likely imposter: best end chops

Giveaway signs:
- a trayful of chops all with rib bones
- too much streaky meat around the eye muscle

Shoulder chops come from the lower part of the chest area, just above the front legs. They are either a tapering oval shape or a very chunky square shape and, like the rest of the shoulder, they are very fatty. They are not often seen since it is easier for the butcher to sell his lamb shoulder as a whole joint. They are so cheap that there is no need for imposters.

Chump chops are cut from the top of the leg, and are the lamb's equivalent of steak. They are round – almost kidney-shaped. Most of the chops have a small round bone on the side, apart from the last one from the joint, where the bone widens out to a thick wedge shape. They may have one or two pockets of fat, but the majority of the chops should be 90 per cent lean.

Likely imposter: shoulder chops

Giveaway signs:
- a trayful of chops which are all fatty
- too long and thin in shape

BEEF STEAKS

Steaks come from the back and side areas between the small of the animal's back, and its tail. But there is nothing to stop a dishonest butcher cutting steaks out of joints from the front end and trimming them to make them look like the real thing. The most likely contenders for this treatment are thick rib and fore-rib joints, which can easily be cut to look like highly sought-after sirloin or rump steaks.

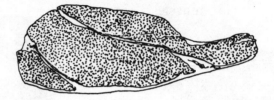

Thick rib joint comes from the front, lower rib area. It is tough, and generally needs stewing or pot-roasting to make it tender. But carefully trimmed, the slices you would normally buy for stews can be made to look remarkably like sirloin to the inexperienced eye. The secret is to look for connective tissue. With the flat, fatty side at the bottom, if you can see a piece of sinew running upwards from one side to the other, then it is not sirloin. This cut is so cheap nothing is likely to be passed off in its place.

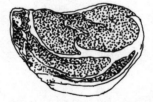

Fore-rib is that popular Sunday roast which resembles the shape of a typical pork chop from the side. Because it is the top, middle part of the back, right next to the sirloin, it is tempting for a butcher to extend his steak-cutting area without lowering the price. Boned and sliced it can make reasonable frying steaks, but they are by no means as tender as either sirloin or rump. All steaks are a chunky oval shape and have a ribbon of white fat making an arc through the centre of the flesh. Again it is cheap, so imposters are unlikely.

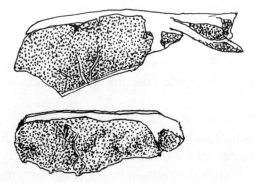

Sirloin joint is found in the lower part of the back, above the rump. If the fillet and bone are left in place it can be chopped into T-bone steaks, but it is most often sold boned as sirloin steaks. They all have a very familiar oval shape – cut short they are almost boat-shaped. The flesh is lean and has no sinew or gristle attached, though it may have a little marbling of fat.

Likely imposters: thick rib slices, fore-rib steaks

Giveaway signs: •   connective tissue running through the lean
              •   ribbons of fat in the meat

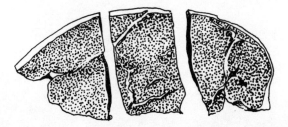

Rump is an odd-shaped wedge in the back and side areas beneath the tail. All the meat is so tender it is almost always cut up into steaks, and because the wedge is over a foot long, it is usually divided up into three, making rump steaks in all different shapes and sizes. At least one of the three steaks will be almost square, since it will have been cut on two sides, and the others should have at least one cut side. The rump does have a few thin ribbons of connective tissue running throughout its length, but there should be no large pockets of fat.

Likely imposters   thick rib slices, fore-rib steaks

Giveaway signs: ● too many identical, oval-shaped pieces
                   ● wide ribbons and pockets of fat

There are many other steaks in a beef carcass, but few of them would be such popular choices for substitution. Fillet steak is so easily recognized by most of us that it is rarely involved in the fiddles, though one butcher was caught trying to pass off 'bola' or 'mock fillet steak', which comes from the chuck-steak region, for the real thing. Of the other frying steaks, topside, silverside and top rump steaks could take the place of rump, but it would hardly be worth the butcher's while. They are too much in demand as Sunday joints. The other 'steaks' are all for stewing – leg, skirt, neck, clod, shin – and because of their very sinewy, fibrous composition they would not be very successful at impersonating the lean steaks . . . but you never know.

Postscript: the campaign for Real Meat

The meat industry will swallow up about £7000 million of our money this year. A tiny part of that will go into the cash tills of some far-sighted entrepreneurs who are trying to bring us a better product.

In an encouraging sign of the times, a few farmers, wholesalers and butchers are trying to provide us with what we really want . . . additive-free meat. As this book goes to press, dozens of butchers shops are due to open selling only meat as it used to be produced. They are buying from farmers who are using the latest scientific know-how combined with traditional methods to produce what can only be called 'real meat'.

They use no hormones and no unnecessary antibiotics or other drugs. The animals are raised naturally, with plenty of open space and fresh air. Slaughterhouses are well designed and use the best methods of stunning, with no pre-slaughter tenderizing allowed. The result is good, flavoursome meat with none of the usual residues.

The shops involved, all independent butchers so far, also boast home-made sausages, packed with lean meat, no fat, and using only natural herbs and spices as flavourings. With so much genuine meat they need no extra colouring, and they sell so fast they do not need preservatives either. Prices will be higher, but only by pennies, and for many of us the extra cost will be well worthwhile.

It is just a shame that the trend has not, at the time of writing, reached the meat product manufacturers, or the supermarkets. Some companies have cut down the fat content of items like sausages in a commendable effort to make them more healthy. This is the first step. But consumers want meat that has no unnecessary water, no flavourings other than herbs and spices, no colourings and no tricks. They want to know that their meat has no drug residues and they need to be assured that the animal was given a good natural life, and treated fairly in death.

If 'real meat' and 'real meat products' catch on like real ale and real wholemeal bread have done, then we can look forward to the sight of more calves in the fields, and the distant memory of pigs rooting in the open will once again become a common sight.

Wouldn't that be a real treat?